MW01064338

Teaching Heartspeak

"This New Breed of Writing"

Ruth Rogers

Heartspeak Publications

Readers may contact the author at

Heartspeak100@gmail.com

ISBN 13: 978-1537607184

ISBN 10: 1537607189

All rights reserved.
Printed in the United States of America.
2016
C

Dedicated to:

All once and future students

in American schools

In gratitude for:

The uncountable number of friends and students

who shared their stories with me

In memory of my parents

Thomas and Mary Katherine Hunter Allis

Contents

Foreword

Moreover, I, on my side, require of every writer, first or last, a simple and sincere account of his own life, and not merely what he has heard of other men's lives. — Henry David Thoreau

"We Know Who Is Writing the Letters."

In 1965, I graduated from Durrett High School in Louisville, Kentucky, and went off to college in Indiana where I met the man who soon became my husband. We abandoned our plans for higher education to begin the adventure of our life together. For the first few years, we lived in a variety of locations, from Kentucky to Tennessee to Alabama and beyond. Hubby wasn't inclined to write letters, so I accepted the role of letter-writer, sharing our lives with his family and mine.

I never had a pen pal and wrote few letters before my marriage. So I relied on my experiences in school to guide me. I tried to write to my husband's relatives in Alabama speaking for both of us. I avoided saying "I" and tried to use "proper" English. This may not sound like a difficult task, but, somehow, I made it so. When his mother wrote, saying, "We know who is writing the letters," I realized his family thought I was trying to trick them.

Now, I am a writing instructor at the university level. When students sign up for my Junior English class, few are strong writers. Most have some of the same confused ideas about writing I once had. They think they should write the formal, higher-level diction students have been taught for generations. In doing so, their writing loses its powerful voice. Trying to write formal or proper English can result in good writing – but rarely does.

The antidote to awkward pompous writing is to write in the language of the heart. Since I haven't found just one word to represent "the language of the heart," I created one: Heartspeak. When students begin following Heartspeak guidelines, their writing often turns around from awkward to powerful, *sometimes overnight*. I call this "the Heartspeak cure."

Of course, my methods do not result in a 100% approval rating with students, but the anonymous comments from students who participated in recent online evaluations of my class reveal my approach differs from what they experienced in other college classes. I often find six or eight hand-written student comments in reply to what is otherwise a fill-in-the-bubble list for the 22 students evaluating each class I teach. Of the hand-written responses, one might be negative. The rest are positive, like those I'm including, here.

Sample End-of-Semester Evaluations

from Anonymous Students

"Ruth Rogers was a wonderful surprise. She has encouraged me to write from the heart. This new breed of writing differs from the stodgy, stuffed shirt, uptight manner in which I had been asked to construct my papers in the past. It has allowed me to say what I truly feel about a variety of subjects and has made this semester a lot of fun."

~~~~

"I loved this class. I loved this class. I loved this class. I would recommend Ruth Rogers to anyone and everyone, because she is fantastic at what she does, and she should continue to do it forever."

~~~~

"I have had many online courses involving writing. I have always had to beg for feedback and most of the time didn't receive it. My previous English instructor didn't grade and post 75% of our material until the week final grades were posted. We didn't have any idea how we were doing and received no feedback. Ruth Rogers has been amazing. We have frequent communication on Blackboard and/or email. She gives plenty of feedback and has not only helped me become a better writer but has helped me enjoy writing as well. The skills I have learned in this class will be an invaluable asset as I begin my upper level classes."

~~~~

"I have loved everything about my English 300 course. I love that the assignments apply to my life. I love that I get to write like I talk. I love that Ruth actually cares about my learning. I love that she gives feedback in a timely manner. I will recommend this class to all of my friends! I have enjoyed it so much that it doesn't seem like school."

~~~~

"I have dreaded this course because I did not enjoy writing. Ruth Rogers has restored my faith in writing and in my ability to write. I have seen a huge improvement in my writing since August. She is very helpful and clear in her assignments and expectations. She has been very upbeat and encouraging to everyone this semester. I'm very glad that I took Ruth for English 300!"

~~~~

"I have recommended Ruth Rogers' online ENG300 course to several students who are as scared of the course as I was. I told them how fun and challenging the class is and how much I have enjoyed it. I actually looked forward to opening up each new assignment. How many instructors have students chomping at the bit to do their homework?"

~~~~

Chapter One

Hard Questions ~ Simple Answers

Be yourself. Above all, let who you are, what you are, what you believe, shine through every sentence you write, every piece you finish. — John Jakes

Questions We Don't Ask — but Should

"Yes! That's exactly how I felt in school!" This is what I thought as I read one of Matt Groening's cartoon strips from his *Life in Hell*. The cartoon frames show a student sitting at his desk. The teacher (heard but not seen) asks, "Any questions, students?" Quietly, the student begins thinking of questions he might ask. Here are some of them.

"Why is school run like a jail?"

"How come you're so boring?"

"Why are there so many stupid rules?"

"Why do we have to use such bland textbooks?"

"How come there is so much emphasis on rote memorization?"

"Why do we have to answer such trivial questions on tests?"

"If a student fails, doesn't that really mean the teacher failed?"

"Why does school have to be this bad?"

Perhaps my reader can identify with Groening's perplexed student. He wonders about the same things maybe we all did. In *Teaching Heartspeak,* I hope my readers find answers to these questions while considering my recommendations on how to bring important changes to the way writing is taught, whether in elementary through high school or in college.

After over a quarter-century of teaching writing in college, I've learned I must, first, help students *put aside* the writing advice they received before coming to college. This "baggage" is a profound handicap. Some students are unable to overcome it.

My main purpose in writing this book is to inspire changes in how we teach writing, beginning in the earliest years of schooling and on through college, so the bad habits students learn and need to abandon after graduating high school are *not taught* them in the first place. Then, instead of remedial instruction in college, students can polish their *good* writing to higher levels of power and eloquence. I dream of a day when this can happen, nation-wide. *It needs to be today.*

At first, my college students find it hard to understand how so much of their previous writing instruction in school could be so wrong. When I introduce the Heartspeak method, sometimes a student will complain, "This goes against everything I've been taught," and others are thinking the same thing. But, if students give "this new breed of writing" a chance, many are amazed when they see how easy powerful writing can be. They find new freedom and confidence as they move beyond their former notions about writing.

Since I mark errors on page one of their first essay and then ask students to try again and revise the whole thing before I assign a grade, students begin seeing their writing through my eyes. But some still struggle giving up old habits. To help them understand the difference, I refer to the older ways as "stinky writing."

The Tradition of Stinky Writing

I'm convinced the usual method of teaching writing — with assigned topics, a focus on explanation, asking for a higher-level of diction than everyday speech, and a required length for written assignments — undermines our birthright of a powerful voice. Let me explain.

Using higher-level diction *creates distance* between the writer's heart and the reader's. This means it is less powerful. And, for most of us, it results in awkward writing. Due to the writing advice we received growing up, we tend to think we sound more intelligent if we don't write like we talk. But I tell students, "Our goal as writers is not to convince readers how intelligent we are. Our goal is to discover our 'voice' and celebrate our passions in writing."

Aristotle wrote, "We are what we repeatedly do. Excellence, then, is not an act but a habit." My attempt to help students put aside their old habits is not always successful. By the time they arrive in my class, some are true believers in the ways of stinky writing and resist change. But many others find a new joy in writing when they learn the ways of Heartspeak.

Not the Teacher's Fault

I do not fault teachers for the problems I see. The culprit is misguided, unchallenged tradition. Whether spoken or implied, "We've always done it this way" brought us to the present state of affairs. We need to recognize the many problems caused by the confused notions about writing that our students pack up and tote along to college.

I have tested Heartspeak guidelines and find them trustworthy. Most students come to my class thinking, "I just want to get this over with and graduate." They tend to believe, "Some people are outstanding writers. I'm just not one of them." This self-assessment handicaps a large percentage of college writers. My desire is to offer them hope, telling them, "All my students can become powerful writers. And it's not hard."

I add, "Just stop doing the bad stuff and there's nothing left to do but the good stuff." This simple mantra helps students regain confidence in their ability to write by challenging them to consider how, buried under layers of bad advice received during their younger years in school, their voice is silenced but survives—waiting to tell their powerful stories. Good writing can flow from the heart, without a struggle, when using Standard American English. It is the foundation for almost all good writing—in or out of college.

The Stairway of Diction

Formal English

Standard American English

Peer Talk

Family Talk

Lovers' Intimate Talk

Babies' Babbling

The Primal Scream

Our speaking or writing voice changes while climbing the stairway of diction. We need to consider our audience when choosing the step we speak or write from. But, for most of life's writing challenges, we should use Standard American English.

Formal writing is not Heartspeak-friendly. Instead, it suggests, "I will enlighten you from the thin air of my intellectual mountaintop." It stands aloof. Can anyone give a good reason to write formal English—except as mock pomposity?

We should tell students, "The measuring stick for the terminology we use in our writing needs to be, 'Will the average person we meet on the street understand this?'" My students who participate in college speech programs tell me they are advised to speak naturally, not with formal diction. *The same advice is long overdue for students of writing.*

Our Thought for Today

I use a teaching device most students enjoy, the Thought for Today. This daily dose of wisdom from writers, philosophers, teachers, and world leaders supports the notion that we have a powerful writing voice, perhaps long obscured. The readers of *Teaching Heartspeak* will find an abundance of those quotations, here, too. Having collected them for decades, I find they have aged like good wine.

Every day and in a variety of ways, traditional methods of teaching writing say, "Use uncommon words and don't write like we talk. Write explanations, not stories." *This does not produce good writing.*

I want students to decide, like Stephen Daedalus in James Joyce's *A Portrait of the Artist as a Young Man,* "I will try to express myself in some mode of life or art as freely as I can and as wholly as I can." This is Heartspeak.

Of Freedom and Trying to Find Ourselves

Students are not sure what to expect when they sign up for college. When I taught Freshman English at Middle Tennessee State University in 1998, a student named Chad wrote, "I remember sitting in class and thinking that college was about freedom and trying to find one's self and this guy was up there explaining where a comma goes."

Students prioritize their reasons for going to college, but learning to write well is rarely among them. Their reasons may include (not necessarily in this order): 1) finding myself, 2) having a good time, 3) being educated in the fine points of a chosen field, 4) graduating with a degree that will increase my earning potential, 5) finding true love, 6) participating in a sports program, 7) getting away from home (independence). These can all be beneficial aspects of the college experience. But when students walk the Heartspeak path to powerful writing, they discover it can help them accomplish *all* their goals for college.

Powerful writing is the most valuable skill college students can acquire, no matter what official degree they seek. Certainly, potential employers should expect college graduates to write well. In her article "Write Brain," in the November, 1997, *Entrepreneur* magazine, Leann Anderson explains, "The ability to write well is not a luxury. It's a necessity. Research has shown that being able to write clearly and concisely, with a minimum of clutter and a dash of originality, can not only save a company money, but it can also enhance the writer's image and career. To be more specific, if you anguish for hours over a memo or report, it can become costly, with no guarantee that the reader will understand the point you're trying to make."

Based on what I've seen of students who take my required English classes, the percent of *college graduates* who have weak writing skills may be as high as 80%. I can say "college graduates" since the majority of my students are nearing graduation from their four-year program. I think those with weak writing skills *could be reduced to perhaps 20%*, if we replace traditional methods of teaching writing with "Heartspeak."

My estimate of weak writers *among high school graduates* could drop from around 95% to 50% or less if traditional methods were replaced with Heartspeak in elementary through high school. These estimates are not based on research studies. They derive from years of experience helping students overcome stinky writing.

Whether college-educated or not, most of us experience some anxiety over how we write. Often, new acquaintances are afraid to send me emails after learning I am an English teacher. The correspondent assumes I am always in "grading mode." I never read casual writing that way. Good writing is not a moral issue, something to judge a person's character by. But it is something more of us should feel confident doing after we graduate high school or college.

We have a place we can go in our minds, in our hearts, where we discover the path to good writing. My goal as a teacher is to help college students walk this pathway often, so they can, after our time together, find it by themselves. The best way I've found to do this is to ask students to write personal narratives.

The Power of Personal Narrative

William Stafford explains, "A writer is not so much someone who has something to say as much as he is someone who has found a process that will bring about new things he would not have thought if he had not started to say them." Flannery O'Conner puts it this way. "I write because I don't know what I think until I see what I say." We may know what we *know*, but until we articulate our beliefs and the life journey that brought us to those beliefs, we are not fully aware of what we *think*. If we write our personal stories, we come to know ourselves in a way we cannot, otherwise. It's why exploring our life experiences in writing is so beneficial.

Maya Angelou reminds us, "There is no greater agony

than bearing an untold story inside you." Telling this untold story can offer inner healing. At the end of a semester, many students thank me for the opportunity to write personal narratives. Sometimes, doing so brings comfort, healing, and catharsis, just as it did for Anne Frank who confided to her diary, "I can shake off everything as I write; my sorrows disappear, my courage is reborn."

Writing personal narratives also helps students learn to write like we talk. Writing about themselves and those close to them is where students begin to appreciate the value of writing from the heart in everyday conversational style. For instance, the character study assignment I give offers obvious reasons to abandon pompous formal writing. Students write about someone close to them, revealing the person's character *by telling stories about what the person loves*. I've found writing powerfully about someone we love is harder to do than most of us realize, until we try it. Matching our words with our emotions is the challenge. Only Heartspeak is suitable for the task.

History ~ Facts or Stories?

In my own days in high school, I was never fond of history class. Now, history is my life. I love delving into family history and celebrating my ancestors. I remember thinking when I was in high school history class, bored with what the textbook offered, "Why don't we just read biographies of the famous people in history?" Instead, the glossed-over textbook approach skims the surface, without revealing the true significance of what happened.

Stories are different. We identify with the main character, and this draws us in. N. Scott Momaday explains, "Stories are pools of reflection in which we see ourselves through the prism of imagination."

It wasn't until after I married and had babies that I began to appreciate how the study of history intersected with the life stories of my own family. Appreciating the significance of my ancestors' experience in the Civil War, for instance, when my great-grandfather, William S. Martin, fought in the Orphan Brigade, helps me understand how such events contribute to my family's passion, pain, and pride — and to who I am.

In *Lies My Teacher Told Me: Everything Your American History Text Got Wrong*, James W. Loewen writes, "History is a furious debate informed by evidence and reason. Textbooks encourage students to believe that history is facts to be learned." He adds, "Fragmenting history into unconnected 'facts' also guarantees, however, that students will not be able to relate many of these terms to their own lives and will retain almost none of them after the six-weeks' grading period."

Loewen reminds us, "American history is full of fantastic and important stories. These stories have the power to spellbind audiences, even audiences of difficult seventh graders."

On occasion, I have read playful approaches to historical events written as though a modern journalist were offering an eye-witness report. A history teacher might invite students to research an event in depth and write an action-packed "I was there" narrative to share with the class. The narratives could be bound into a class collection. If each student is given a copy, it will become a unique reminder of the class and the time period in history being studied.

The time-traveling reporter project is a way student writers can develop their talent without feeling any need for formal diction. It is story-based. In addition to descriptive detail, the student can express surprise, disgust, or envy when encountering the customs of the period of history he or she visits—along with reporting on some historical event. And dialogue should be included. Heartspeak storytelling is not limited to English composition classes. It's a method we can rely on for all writing challenges. What a shame that educators for generations have suggested students leave their heart at the door when entering most classrooms.

Chapter Two

"Dearly Beloved, We Are Gathered Here, Today"

I wanted to be as they were telling me I should be, so I ceased to exist; I had renounced my soul's private obligations.
– Rosario Ferré

Most of us learned the Ten Commandments of Stinky Writing in our days in elementary through high school. They were implied, if not stated. By discouraging us from writing in our normal voice, they become pallbearers at the funeral for powerful writing. By now, my readers may have noticed I happily break the Ten Commandments of Stinky Writing, myself.

The Ten Commandments of Stinky Writing

1. Thou shalt not have "I" (or other first person pronouns) in your writing.

2. Thou shalt not use contractions in your writing, such as "can't," "won't," "haven't," "it's."

3. Thou shalt not end a sentence with a preposition, such as "What is it made of?"

4. Thou shalt not begin a sentence with any of the seven coordinating conjunctions, namely: "for," "and," "nor," "but," "or," "yet," "so." (Acronym: FANBOYS.)

5. Thou shalt not write like we talk. Instead, consult a thesaurus and use smarter-sounding uncommon words.

6. Thou shalt not write about religion or other controversial issues, revealing bias.

7. Thou shalt analyze, explain, and persuade—but avoid telling stories from your life.

8. Thou shalt avoid honest emotion. Write from the head, not from the heart.

9. Thou shalt wait for a teacher to tell you how to write, rather than trusting your own judgment about length, tone, and style.

10. Thou shalt write on assigned topics, pretending you care about them when you don't.

Since the rules for stinky writing keep us from writing like we talk, *they are a not-so-subtle rejection of who we are.* We need to reject them! They discourage us from writing in the language of the heart. Through returning to a storytelling foundation and using conversational English, we can find our voice and soar on strengthened linguistic wings, whatever genre we write in. A line from the movie *Arabian Knights* reminds us, "People need stories more than life, itself. They tell us how to live and why."

Heartspeak ~ Powerful, Not Stinky

By celebrating our lives in personal narratives, we develop powerful writing skills more easily than in explanatory writing. Perhaps this is *because we learned all those stinky writing rules while writing explanation* (sometimes referred to as "exposition," "analysis," or "argument."). It helps to take a new, less stinky approach.

Consider the following quotations. One is in pompous formal style, the other more like we talk. Both invite the reader to put aside judging when trying to understand others.

~~~~

Formal writing: *"A true and full understanding of another's thought is possible only when we understand the affective volitional basis."* — L. S. Vygotsky, in *Thought and Language*

~~~~

Writing like we talk: *"Grant that I may not criticize my neighbor until I have walked a mile in his moccasins."* – Native American Prayer

~~~~

The main difference in these two examples is every word in the second one will be understood by anyone who grew up speaking English. This is not true of the first example. And it is awkward. We need to write in language the average person will understand.

Three Strikes and Your Voice Is Out!

Before college (and in college), most students are asked to use what they come to think of as "smarter sounding" words for writing. Through the use of a thesaurus and various formal writing models, students are told, "Use higher-level diction."

Last semester, I did a survey of students in the college English classes I teach. Those who responded said no other teacher in high school or college asked them to "write like we talk." But they said teachers in high school and (or) college *did* ask them to use a thesaurus.

The push to use higher-level diction and write with words we don't use every day is **the first nail in the coffin of our writing voice.** And it suggests our conversational voice is "not good enough." This becomes a dead-end detour, leading us away from the most reliable route to powerful writing.

Many elementary through high school teachers insist students write on assigned topics rather than writing about something the student has an interest in. This is **the second nail in the coffin of voice.**

After years of being told what to write about, rather than being encouraged to write the stories of their lives or explore topics they have an interest in, some students arrive in college classes unaware if they even have an interest they might want to explore in writing. They expect the teacher to provide a topic.

Most elementary, middle, and high school teachers ask students to write a required number of words or pages, rather than allowing them to develop a *sense* for when they have told their stories well or fully explored a topic before bringing closure.

Even worse, when given a goal of a certain number of words or pages, students are hesitant to remove unnecessary words and phrases when editing. *Each word "counts" towards the total length.* Student writers are tempted to borrow too much from other sources or even plagiarize when given length requirements. So a required number of words or pages is **the third nail in the coffin of voice.**

When my students receive their first assignment, they ask me, "How many pages does this have to be?"

I tell them, "Even though I don't require a minimum number of pages, less than three double-spaced pages is usually insufficient development." If they decide to give me just one or two pages, their grade may suffer due to lack of detail and development in the writing. But I have seen the rare excellent student essay written in two pages, even, one time, in one page. So I leave the decision to students. If they write too little, their grade will reflect their choice.

I want students to develop an appreciation for when they have written enough, been generous with detail and dialogue, and should bring closure. If never given the opportunity to make such choices, how will they learn? The only length requirement in my class is for the research paper. But, instead of the ten-page requirement for our research paper, one student a few years ago wrote fourteen pages while celebrating her topic. It was fourteen pages of passion.

When students are encouraged to discover and write about topics they care about in their essays, most enjoy writing and go beyond the three-page suggested minimum. This past semester, our second assignment was titled, "Create Your Own Assignment." In the instructions, I offered a long list of anecdotal quotations to inspire student writers. They chose one reminding them of a story from their lives. Or, if they had another quotation they preferred, they used their own favorite, placing the quotation below the essay title, as an epigraph. Some students went several pages beyond the recommended minimum. Choosing their own topic generated deep emotions, and they had much to say.

However, since the crippling trinity of writing instructions I refer to as "Three Strikes and Your Voice is Out" along with the "Ten Commandments of Stinky Writing" are part of the traditional method for teaching writing, they undermine students' opportunities to discover their voices and their own reasons for writing. Instead, student writers are rewarded for pretending an interest in assigned topics and writing what become long, awkward sentences with unnecessary words.

Psychologists specializing in education should have pointed to the harm caused by the guidelines for stinky writing generations ago. Maybe they did and we were not paying attention. Students who are taught the traditional ways accept them without resistance. They are told, "This is what you need to know for college." Their teachers attended college. They should know. Right?

The burden of "This is the way it has always been done" can prevent us from making necessary course corrections in life's journey. This is why the inertia of tradition is so overwhelming. Every day of every semester while reading student writing, I see the need for change, the need to stop teaching the formal approach damaging students' writing.

When I met with one student she explained, "I want to write like I talk, but I was so traumatized by my English professor last semester that I have a hard time turning off his voice in my head." Tradition and trauma are frequent visitors in the college classroom.

The Hand-Me-Down Methods

The prevailing methods of teaching writing from elementary through high school are in opposition to what even a basic understanding of psychology should reveal about helping writers improve. But the weight of tradition seduces educators to ignore what should be obvious by now. I call the harmful writing traditions, "The hand-me-down methods," since this is the way writing has been taught for generations. If it produces such poor results, why continue?

Reinforcement for the hand-me-down methods may come from parents, too. They struggled in school trying to write proper English. So they may think it their duty to encourage their children who are struggling with the same thing, like some rite of passage. Instead, parents need to question the whole process. But the weight of tradition causes us to accept the status quo.

Since the hand-me-down methods ask us to write a different dialect than we speak, students may think, "If I just write sentences different from everyday speech, they will be good sentences." Of course, this is not true. It results in a game of "How can I avoid writing like I talk? Let me count the ways." And 99 out of 100 attempts are awful.

Years ago, when I was a student worker in our college Writing Center, I helped a young man improve his essay. He wrote what were fairly clear sentences, except each had an uncommon word that did not make sense in context. So I asked, "Why did you use this word?"

His reply, "Well, I just thought it sounded better."

When I asked what the uncommon words meant, he didn't know. So I teased him, saying, "Did you just tape a list of 'big' words to the wall and throw a dart, then plug that word into your sentence?" His reply was a sheepish grin. But most of the writing I saw while helping at the Writing Center was equally confused.

Propositions We Agree Not to Question

Teaching children in elementary through high school is one of the hardest jobs anyone can have. I know college instructors who tried it, only to discover they could not endure the hours, stress, and enormous responsibility the teachers of America's youth face every day. So they scurried back to teach at the university.

If those who teach our children try teaching the Heartspeak method, they will discover a more successful approach, once students find more confidence and joy in writing. We can no longer ignore the need to replace the hand-me-down tradition of teaching writing based on something other than the way we talk.

Vine Deloria, Jr., writes in *Spirit and Reason*, "Western civilization seems to have a multitude of 'commonsense' propositions, and as common sense is such a rarity, what we actually mean by this statement is that we have a certain set of propositions that we have agreed not to question." This is the trap of tradition.

Generation after generation, teachers give children and teens the same hand-me-down writing instruction the teachers themselves were given in elementary through high school. Even if they think some of it is bad advice, it tends *not* to get corrected. But when those who teach our children begin understanding the potential power of Heartspeak— *in their own writing*—the change will come.

A powerful voice is not a luxury, not just an option. Human authenticity is contingent upon it. And how is authenticity connected to our voice—whether speaking or writing? Rollo May explains, "If you do not express your own original ideas, if you do not listen to your own being, you will have betrayed yourself."

Why Wait?

If the traditional way of teaching writing is going to be replaced, our children's teachers need to discover their own powerful writing voices. Colleges of education need to turn away from encouraging formal writing and begin offering a required "Heartspeak Writing" class for all future teachers. Even if this does not happen immediately, *Teaching Heartspeak* can become a teacher's guide. Determined teachers can begin making a difference, now. Happy students will spread the word. Old traditions will begin to crumble.

Even with existing writing programs in place in elementary through high school, the shift away from stinky writing can be accomplished by teachers rejecting the Ten Commandments of Stinky Writing and the harm done by Three Strikes and Your Voice is Out. Teachers can learn this new breed of writing by experimenting with it *along with* their students.

Vivian Gussin Paley is quoted in Linda Winston's *Keepsakes*, saying, "There should be a sign above every classroom door that reads, 'All teachers who enter, be prepared to tell your story.'" I model Heartspeak storytelling for students by writing my own stories as examples for some of their assignments and by sharing anecdotes from my life in frequent messages to my online classes. I also share examples of Heartspeak essays from former students (with their permission).

I encourage all elementary, middle, and high school teachers to *begin now* writing your own life stories. Spend a summer doing it—between school years—*if not before*. After you begin, stories will bubble up from your subconscious, begging to be told. This is what happened as I wrote my master's thesis—a collection of stories from my life.

Sue Monk Kidd offers another reason for telling our stories when she writes, "Stories have to be told or they die, and when they die, we can't remember who we are or why we're here."

College Teachers Can Begin Now, Too

College teachers don't need to wait for elementary through high school teachers to train the next generation of college bound students to write from the heart. In some ways, college teachers have more freedom than elementary, middle, and high school teachers. We can begin a Heartspeak intervention program in our classrooms, *immediately*.

I know of no college textbook that recommends teaching the Ten Commandments of Stinky Writing or the methods of Three Strikes and Your Voice is Out. College teachers who learned them as children reinforce the same ideas in their students. But we can abandon them at any time. After generations of these traditions doing such harm to our powerful writing voice, we need to say, "Enough!"

Teaching should be a heart-to-heart creative activity. What Winston Churchill said applies well to teaching: "We make a living by what we get, but we make a life by what we give." Great teachers give their heart.

Chapter Three

First Steps on the Path to Heartspeak

I wish the college I bound my identity over to had introduced me to my heart. —Jane Tompkins

Heartspeak ~ The Basics

1) Write like we talk. (The first person "I" is welcome.)

2) Tell a story. (Your own *true* story.)

3) Be concise. (Remove any word that, if removed, does not change the basic message of the sentence.)

Early in my journey toward understanding what life is about, I discovered a claim that may seem self-evident. It goes something like this: To become good or competent at any endeavor, we need to understand two things, the theory and the practice. The three steps I offer above tell how to practice Heartspeak. But polishing the three steps is essential, too.

The sub-title of this book, "This New Breed of Writing," is a phrase I found in one of the student evaluations in my foreword. *Heartspeak is new to students.* But it's not new to our most popular published writers. They know where the power is and what people will pay to read.

For generations, academics have rejected writing like we talk in favor of formal writing. But anyone who writes for a living knows better. An Internet search will reveal the methods I teach are what they recommend. (Look up "quotations on writing.")

Sadly, what professional writers have known for generations hasn't found its way into most classrooms. Albert Camus reminds us, "Those who write clearly have readers. Those who write obscurely have commentators." This is my rationale for teaching Heartspeak. Down with obscure writing!

Discovering Heartspeak

As a graduate student working on a master's degree, and, later, in a doctoral program, I tested the ideas I am teaching now. I found story-based writing, concise and like we talk, was well received by my professors. They found nothing to complain about in my conversational way of writing with anecdotal personal stories. My professors recommended I submit papers to various journals for publication.

While teaching two classes of Freshman English each semester as a graduate assistant, I became convinced the write-like-we-talk foundation is what my students needed, too. And students have responded enthusiastically to it in my classrooms ever since. But, when they arrive in my classes, most believe they need to write formal, stodgy English. It can take a while to convince them otherwise.

Fear of Writing

I explain the simple steps for writing Heartspeak the first week of class. But, since students have been trying to do something else for all their years in school, few can change overnight. Even having my guidelines and frequent online reminders, some struggle giving up long-held ideas.

The artificial, higher-level diction asked of students in elementary through high school does more to turn them against writing than anything else. When students do not enjoy writing, they avoid it. Is this the result our education system wants to achieve—fear and dislike of writing?

Perhaps nothing is more damaging to the mental and emotional development of most school children than the boredom they experience in school. And boredom mixed with confusion over how to write can lead to fear of writing. In *Actual Minds, Possible Worlds*, Jerome Bruner writes, "Boredom has always played more of a role in human history than we are prepared to admit. And we should never underrate the boredom induced by empty ideas pretentiously paraded."

The Junior English class I teach is one of the required writing classes. Many students put it off as long as possible— due to a fear of writing and dreading the required research paper. Putting off the Junior English class is not wise, but students often take my class the final semester before graduation. They could benefit from it more by taking it as sophomores.

When students who were taught the rules for stinky writing take my class, most are afraid to write and have no idea what their writing voice sounds like. Some experience writer's block, and say, "I sat at the computer for hours, unable to think of anything to write." So I encourage them to break through this mental paralysis by writing *about* the frustration of writer's block in their first assignment for my class — a history of the student's experiences as a writer.

From "Proper" to "Powerful"

Students regain hope when I tell them their previous writing instruction may be the cause of their problems. This message helps them put aside the notion that writing just isn't their gift. It helps them begin telling their powerful stories with renewed confidence in their ability. Boredom is no longer a problem when they are given the opportunity to explore and celebrate their own lives in narrative essays.

I also tell students, "Except you become as a little child, you might not be a very good writer." Little children speak from the heart — in unsophisticated honesty. When we recapture the UN-self-conscious voice we had before we encountered the rules of stinky writing, we reclaim our birthright. According to Baudelaire, "Genius is simply childhood rediscovered by an act of will."

Students need to write in their own conversational voice about something they care about. No set length. No set topic. And no BS. "Say what you mean and mean what you say!" They are a bit unsettled at first, but when they rediscover their voice, they love it. Some even write letters to me at the end of the semester saying writing Heartspeak and having an encouraging reader helped them find an outlet for the turmoil inside.

I want students to do *for me* as C. S. Lewis says (of himself), "Think of me as a fellow patient in the same hospital, who, having been admitted a little earlier, could give some advice." I needed the Heartspeak cure, too.

The Sometimes "Overnight Cure"

I recall many students' struggles to put aside the proper prescription they learned for writing. One sweet lady, a young grandmother, wrote awkward, confused essays due to thinking she needed to use uncommon formal words and write long sentences. One day, I called her into my office and gently went over her latest essay, line by line, showing her how to convert confused sentences into clear English. Before she left, I suggested she write her next essay about her childhood experiences growing up on the farm—"exactly as you might tell it to your eight-year-old granddaughter."

Wide-eyed and surprised, she asked, "Exactly as I'd tell my granddaughter?"

"Yes!" I replied. "Imagine you are talking to her as you write. And then read it aloud to check for conversational flow."

My student agreed to try it. Her next essay was wonderful! Almost overnight, she had the Heartspeak cure. And her writing continued to improve throughout the semester. Her reluctance to write like she talked had blocked the flow of powerful writing. Many students experience a similar cure when they are willing to lay aside previous ideas of "good" writing and begin writing like we talk.

If I had to choose only one story to illustrate the importance of writing like we talk, it must be the one about a young man from Eritrea, North Africa. He was in my Freshman English class at Middle Tennessee State University. He was around 26 years old and spoke perfect English. But he wrote tortured sentences in essays for class, until one day when he sat down next to me at a computer in the writing lab.

We talked awhile. The young man explained his main goal in taking Freshman English was to improve his skills, since he volunteered to help other Eritrean immigrants fill out their applications to stay in America. When his parents brought him to America as a child, he attended Catholic schools, but he never learned to write well. He could speak perfect English, due to learning it as a child. And, in my class, he heard me say many times, "Just write like we talk." But he still struggled.

After we talked a few minutes in the lab, I returned to writing at my computer, and the young man began working on an essay at the next computer. After he wrote the first sentence, he asked what I thought. As usual, the writing was jumbled and confusing. So I asked him to read it aloud. Amazingly, the words he spoke as he read were perfect English—very different from the words he wrote.

I said, "Do you realize the words you are speaking do not match the words you typed?"

"Yes," he said.

So I added, "If you will just read aloud what you write—correcting the words on the screen to match the words you are speaking as you did just now—they will be correct."

It was a "light bulb moment" for the young man. He began making changes. Soon, his sentence was perfect. Then he wrote another sentence—and did the same thing—and another. I was thrilled! He had "the cure," finally realizing I meant what I said with, "Write like we talk." His 20-plus years of writing problems were cured in a few moments.

I have had the joy and honor to see this transformation

take place many times over the years. It feels like being a mid-wife at the birth of a new writer. It is life-changing. The writer is saying goodbye to the old fears and writing anxieties while welcoming a newfound expressive freedom.

Award Winning Writing

Another student I had at MTSU was non-traditional, older than most. She was afraid to write with Heartspeak guidelines. She said it went against everything she had been taught. So I told her to discuss it with other instructors before she tried it in their classes. She began taking baby steps in this way of writing, and, by the end of the semester, she won one of three English Department awards for student writing. In fact, that semester, two of the three awards (the top prize of $500 and third prize of $100) went to my freshmen. And other students in my classes have won awards over the years by applying Heartspeak guidelines, too.

Students hear me say, "Write like we talk," but some have a hard time believing I mean what I say. The memories of all their years trying to write proper English for school are like a cancer needing to be surgically removed before they can relax and write from the heart.

When, at last, they discover the power of Heartspeak, students can experience what Lucy Calkins describes in *Living Between the Lines,* "Being human means we can remember and tell story and pretend and write and hope and share, and in this way we add growth rings of meaning to our lives."

Writing like we talk is not "dumbing down" our writing. The rhythms of everyday speech bring an uncommon vitality to writing. Stodgy is replaced with Heartspeak.

It is important to emphasize the "we," in "like *we* talk." *I am not asking for the idiosyncrasies of the dialect of an individual student.* Slang, cussing, and clichés arc not welcome, except in dialogue. And, even there, cussing needs to be converted to a nonsense combination of letters and symbols.

A strict adherence to form is not always necessary. We can mix genres—essay, poetry, journaling, and others. And, for anyone who aspires to be a fiction writer, writing true stories from the heart is the pathway to powerful fiction writing, too. Often, the writings of well-known fiction authors are a fanciful expansion on their own experiences.

Consider Patrick Henry's famous statement: "I know not what course others may take. But as for me, give me liberty or give me death!" We sometimes think this is the pinnacle of eloquence. But it has nothing in common with the dispassionate diction many students and some teachers believe should be characteristic of college writing. Higher-level pompous diction undermines passion. Heartspeak and eloquence are twins of the same mother.

Storytelling as the Foundation of Communication

Telling our own stories is the way we learn to talk as children and the way we share our hearts throughout our lives. This makes stories the foundation of powerful communication.

Since our days in school tend to focus on the mind more than the emotions, my challenge to write from the heart may tug student writers out of their comfort zone. To write powerfully, I encourage them to *not* try to distance what they write from their feelings.

For instance, some want to use the pronoun "one" (as in, "One sees this challenge as a way to. . ."). Instead, I ask them to write in first person, something previous teachers may have forbidden.

Obviously, the sound of talking is prominent in Heartspeak, since it is based on writing like we talk. But the sound of talking is emphasized in other ways, such as when we include dialogue in stories. Quoted dialogue can work to make *exposition* lively, too. The skills we learn to use in storytelling can be employed to improve all forms of writing.

Walter J. Ong insists storytelling is the form of communication underlying all others. He writes in *Orality and Literacy*, "In a sense narrative is paramount among all verbal art forms because of the way it underlies so many other art forms. . . . Behind even the abstractions of science there lies narrative of the observations on the basis of which the abstractions have been formulated. . . . The elemental way to process human experience verbally is to give an account of it, more or less as it really comes into being and exists, embedded into the flow of time."

Ong's praise for narrative could influence the way we create textbooks, especially for a university's college of education program preparing teachers for their interactions with students. The desire to teach Heartspeak will be encouraged by asking future teachers to use its three basic steps while writing personal narratives about their own days in school. Interviewing others to learn about the many ways students develop a fear of writing will help, too.

Story-based Textbooks

Those who write textbooks need to consider Ong's insight about the way storytelling allows us to "process human experience verbally" by giving "an account of it, more or less as it really comes into being." Textbook writing can be elevated from mundane to celebratory if story, humor, and surprise are blended with the necessary informative data by authors who are encouraged to add their own stories, revealing the source of their passion for the subject.

Normally, we do not think of textbooks for the sciences (or other fields) written in narrative. But narrative connects the dots between facts in a way exposition alone cannot do, making the main points more memorable. In her Nobel Prize acceptance speech, Toni Morrison remarked, "Narrative has always been more than mere enjoyment for me. It's the primary way I absorb knowledge." I suspect narrative is the primary way *anyone* absorbs knowledge.

Barbara Hardy, in *Tellers and Listeners* writes, "Humankind cannot bear very much abstraction or discursive reasoning." In *Novel*, Fall, 1968, Hardy describes narrative's pervasive presence in our lives, saying, "We dream in narrative, day-dream in narrative, remember, anticipate, hope, despair, believe, doubt, plan, revise, criticize, construct, gossip, learn, hate, and love by narrative."

Our writing for school and for everything else will be more powerful if we follow the storytelling path. Virginia Woolf took this path and referred to her preference for narrative, saying, "So, if you will allow me, instead of analysing (sic) and abstracting, I will tell you a simple story" (from "Mr. Bennett and Mrs. Brown").

Finding Our Voice

For most of us, the word "story," suggests "fiction." Childhood's bedtime stories are often make-believe. And parents sometimes say, when they suspect a child is not being truthful, "Are you telling a story?" So we grow up thinking of tall tales or fictional classics when we hear the word "story."

Likewise, if a child in elementary school is told to write a story, he or she assumes it should be fiction. If the teacher wants a true story, this requires further explanation. In college the same holds true. Students know the Creative Writing class focuses on writing poems, short stories and, sometimes, longer works of fiction. The required composition classes and literature classes rarely ask for personal narratives. Instead, they focus on analysis and on the persuasive writing we refer to as "arguments."

The typical college student has little opportunity to develop narrative writing skills—whether as fiction or non-fiction—without signing up for a creative writing or an autobiography class. The former is more popular than the latter. Sometimes autobiography classes are canceled for not having the required number of students. The deep wells of wonderful word-craft so easily discovered through writing personal narratives go untapped. But a greater loss is the opportunity for student writers to discover what John J. Erickson reminds us of by saying, "It is through our accumulated stories that we all have our identities."

Those students who write for college and never discover their natural writing voice miss out on a direct path to "finding myself"—one of their main expectations for the college experience. The self-conscious search for "Who am I?" is derailed when required writing classes offer little opportunity for students to write about their lives.

I recall a young man in one of my Freshman English classes whose writing was outstanding. The day he came to my office for a one-on-one session, I said, "Your writing is the best in the class. You have a gift."

He sat quietly, thinking about what I said, then wistfully replied, "Why didn't my high school teachers ever tell me this? I might have chosen a different major in college."'

I could not tell my student why his high school teachers overlooked his talent for writing, but maybe it was due to the traditional way teachers choose the topic and length of student essays in high school and may never ask students to write about their passions.

We *Need* Stories

Sharing the stories of our lives is the way we interact with friends and family. Being encouraged to do this in writing, too, is important. Otherwise, *we develop two voices* — the one for speaking from the heart, the other for writing from the head. But celebrating who we are relies on storytelling. Schooling at any age or level misses an opportunity to offer students powerful encounters with writing by asking them to always write from the head, in explanation.

As writers, we need to help our reader see the events of story through our eyes. This means we need to *show* what happened, using past tense verbs (for past actions), with detail, and dialogue. We *show* what we might otherwise explain. Explanation can cover the same territory, but not as powerfully.

Author Virginia Woolf, at age thirteen, suffered a profound loss in the death of her mother. Afterwards, she was obsessed by the memory of her mother, until, at age forty-four, she wrote *To the Lighthouse*. Later she explained, "I wrote the book very quickly; and when it was written, I ceased to be obsessed by my mother. . . . I suppose I did for myself what psychoanalysts do for their patients. I expressed some long felt and deeply felt emotion. And in expressing it, I explained it and laid it to rest." Her comment is found in *Moments of Being: Unpublished Autobiographical Writings*, edited by Jeanne Schulkind. The act of expressing "some long felt and deeply felt emotion" and laying it to rest is what students often experience when writing their autobiographical narratives.

One of the most memorable student evaluations of my class said, "For the first time in my life I enjoy writing. I am not scared of failing and I have learned a lot since I started writing from the heart. Sometimes in school we become like robots over time. I think that school was probably meant to allow people to reflect, think in depth about their interests or passions. Somewhere along the line if you are not careful you end up selling your soul for a degree or just to be done with the long process. However, if your heart is not in whatever you are doing in life, you will be miserable and lost."

William Faulkner's Nobel Prize acceptance speech underscores what the student above was saying and the way he (or she) said it. Faulkner writes, "The problems of the human heart in conflict with itself . . . alone can make good writing because only that is worth writing about, worth the agony and the sweat."

Facing My Own Fear of Writing

I was in the final semester of working towards a master's degree in English when I signed up for a Creative Writing class at Western Kentucky University. I was one of only six students in the class — all girls.

On the first day, our professor asked us to write a personal introduction to read to the class at our next session. He wanted us get to know each other. But I was overcome with fear. I didn't want to look back at my painful past, even if it meant the end of my time at the university. I was not afraid of writing, per se. But, even though my teacher didn't say, "Write about your deepest pain," I didn't want to pull the scab off the wound created by the loss of my marriage of over twenty years to the father of my three sons.

After a long, tear-filled weekend of inner struggle, I came up with a plan. I would write a *fictional* autobiography. I even gave this fiction a name—my "naughto-biography," since it was "naughty" to alter the professor's assignment. But he had a sense of humor. I knew he would understand.

At our next class, I read the preposterous story to my six classmates and our amazed professor. I said my parents were missionaries killed in Africa during the Mau Mau uprising, while I was hiding under their bed. I escaped by stowing away on a freighter bound for Germany where I became a house guest of the family of a new friend, Priscilla, (later "Priscilla Presley.")

After making it through that first assignment, I overcame my fear and wrote personal narratives the rest of the semester. It was so liberating that I decided to write my master's thesis as a collection of stories from my life. I have encouraged my own students to write their true stories, ever since.

Concise Writing

According to Thomas Jefferson, "The most valuable of all talents is that of never using two words when one will do." We need to *remove every word we can*, if doing so does not undermine the message, the grammar, or the way we talk.

And the challenge can be fun— a game we win if we discover every unnecessary word. Having more words than necessary "waters down" the power of our writing. Like ice melting in a fizzy drink, it spoils the flavor.

Examples of Editing to Be Concise

1) We can replace two words with one—sometimes more specific and accurate.

> a) Students have little motivation to *hang onto* the information.
>
> b) Students have little motivation to *retain* the information.

2) We can replace negative words like "no," "none," "not" with positive ones. Readers respond better to a positive statement than a negative one.

> a) Students take many classes, while *not quite sure whether* the classes will have a practical application outside of academia.
>
> b) Students take many classes, while *remaining unconvinced if* the classes will have a practical application outside of academia.

3) When using two words that mean much the same thing, we can keep the better one and remove the other.

> a) Words like "appositives," "participial phrases," and "subordinate clauses," are *uncommon or nonexistent* in

everyday life.

b) Words like "appositives," "participial phrases," and "subordinate clauses," are *uncommon* in everyday life.

4) We can fine tune phrases to use fewer words.

a) In college, we *think maybe* few of our classes *will offer information that is* pertinent to our life goals.

b) In college, we *suspect* few of our classes *will be* pertinent to our life goals.

5) We can revise unwieldy sentences for clarity.

a) We can *get busy doing that without introducing the process by dissecting it.*

b) We can *do it without dissecting the process.*

6) We can replace a word of two or more syllables or four or more letters with one having fewer syllables or fewer letters.

a) I didn't want to pull the scab off the wound left *from* the *failure* of my marriage.

b) I didn't want to pull the scab off the wound left *by* the *loss* of my marriage.

7) We can remove implied referential words.

a) I said my parents were missionaries *who were killed* in Africa during the Mau Mau uprising.

b) I said my parents were missionaries *killed* in Africa during the Mau Mau uprising.

These are just a few examples of how to "use fewer words."

It may seem nit-picky, but editing every sentence to be concise has a positive cumulative effect in improving our writing.

Eliminating UNNECESSARY words is the purpose of concise writing. But don't misunderstand. Long sentences are fine, if they occur as a result of being concise and offering specifics.

Be Specific

What do I mean by "specific"? Here are three examples of editing weak, "so what" sentences to become more specific.

Weak Version:

I went to the store and bought cookies.

Better Version:

While shopping at Kroger, I bought Royal Dansk butter cookies.

Best Version:

While shopping for after Christmas bargains at Kroger, I bought a year's supply of my favorite Royal Dansk butter cookies at half price and put them in my freezer.

Chapter Four

Teaching "Write Like We Talk" — Like We Talk

Example is not the main thing in influencing others. It is the only thing. — Albert Schweitzer

I agree with French-born American historian, Jacques Barzun, when he says in *Begin Here: The Forgotten Conditions of Teaching and Learning*, "If instead of always using the jargon word 'skills,' school people used the word 'power,' they might judge the result of their teaching more concretely. They would see that passing a fill-in test in English composition means nothing if the passer is powerless — not able — to write ten lines of prose." Barzun refers to "skills" as a jargon word, but, especially when teaching grammar, teachers use jargon words many students' brains resist.

English novelist Zadie Smith writes, "English, as a subject, never really got over its upstart nature. It tries to bulk itself up with hopeless jargon and . . . tries to imitate subjects it can never be." Teaching new concepts does not require we use strange new words students are likely to forget. For instance: "transitive" and "intransitive." What do those mean?

I manage to make few grammatical errors when writing — but my brain has no fondness for remembering the formal terminology of grammar. Instead I take a "like we talk" approach to teaching comma use. I give students ten basic comma uses with names based on a snippet of dialogue related to the comma's function. Here are the first three.

~~~~

1) The *"Hey you!"* comma follows a name, title, noun, or second person pronoun ("you") found as the first word of a sentence, when someone is spoken to directly.

   Examples:

   John, shut the door.

   Lady, do you need an umbrella?

~~~~

2) The *"Hello!"* comma follows an introductory word or phrase and separates it from the main thought of a sentence.

   Examples:

   Today, I hope to get out of the doctor's office before dark.

   Whenever I'm feeling blue, I sing "Summertime."

~~~~

3) The *"Excuse me!"* comma comes as a set, one preceding and one following a word or phrase interrupting the main thought of a sentence.

   Examples:

   When I go to the grocery, as I do each Thursday, I look

for bargains.

"Yes," Nathan said, "the Monopoly game belongs to me.

~~~~

Forgetting the Term Means Forgetting the Skill?

The student who remembers new terminology easily, perhaps one with a scientific or mathematical "bent," may find it easy to remember the terms English teachers use to label the landscape of grammar. However, I suspect most students find such terms difficult to remember. And, when they forget the terms, they may also forget the skills.

Teaching writing in everyday terminology is not hard to do. We can avoid the traditional nomenclature and still teach the skill related to it with a simple "good stuff" — "bad stuff" checklist. When compared side by side, the reason we prefer good stuff should become self-evident. I offer tips for avoiding common errors this way in the writing checklist I give students. It is a jargon-free zone.

Students hope that someday, somewhere, a teacher will say the right words and all will become clear. They will be cured of their confusion. After at least twelve years of writing instruction in elementary and secondary school, if traditional methods worked, my students would not still be struggling to feel competent in writing. It pleases me the way many do find a cure for their confusion in my classes.

Are High School Teachers Prepared to Teach Writing? The ERIC web site summarizes an article found in the *Journal of Educational Psychology*, volume 101, February 2009, by Sharlene A. Kjuhara, Steve Graham, and Leanne S. Hawken. The article is titled, "Teaching Writing to High School Students: A National Survey."

The ERIC summary says of the survey, "Most teachers did not believe their college teacher education program adequately prepared them to teach writing. A sizable minority of language arts and social studies teachers indicated that their in-service preparation was inadequate too." So, assuming the 2009 study would resemble today's results, we have an under-prepared group of graduates from colleges of education taking on the task of teaching writing to young folks in high school on the verge of going off to college, themselves.

Holly Robinson writes, "The first rule to follow when evaluating teachers should be the same one we use in medicine. Teachers, like doctors, should first, do no harm." Teachers do the best they can. But centuries of public schooling should have prepared us to do better at following the "First, do no harm" mandate. A harmful malaise of confusion and anxiety about writing plagues most students who go off to college.

Teachers Are Victims, Too.

For over 30 years, I saved an article written by Erma Bombeck, published in newspapers December 1, 1983, titled, ". . . and teach Johnny to read, if you have any time left." In it Bombeck discusses the many other tasks elementary school teachers are asked to fulfill during class time, while teaching Johnny to read. Among her numerous examples, Bombeck includes, "And you'll have to make time to build economic awareness, assist in bladder control, stress bilingual development and eliminate sex discrimination." Elementary school teachers have had my deepest sympathies ever since I read Bombeck's assessment.

My sympathy for elementary through high school teachers increases when I consider how "the system" is self-perpetuating. In his essay, "Against School," John Taylor Gatto writes, "Of course, teachers are themselves products of the same twelve-year compulsory school programs that so thoroughly bore their students, and as school personnel they are trapped inside structures even more rigid than those imposed upon the children."

I'm reminded of the old Milton Berle TV show. Ruth Gilbert, who played Berle's scatterbrained secretary, "Max," always said in their skits, "It's bigger than both of us, Uncle Miltie." Likewise, tradition is bigger than all of us and hard to resist. But we must do so, if we want the best for our children.

In "Freshman Composition: The Circle of Unbelief," (included in Kenneth G. Wilson's *The Play of Language*) William E. Coles, Jr., says, "Teachers of English Composition go on using methods and materials which were obsolete ten years ago, a hundred years ago, ten centuries ago." It is time to bring the hand-me-down method of teaching to a halt.

A Necessary Evil?

Students consider required college writing classes a necessary evil. They just want to jump through the hoops and put the classes behind them. But a Heartspeak overhaul can change this, *as student comments in my foreword demonstrate*. Such an overhaul can prevent the paralysis of voice students experience and help them find a new joy in writing.

Finding an immediate solution to the crisis is urgent. The road to formal writing we have traveled for so long is full of pot holes, breaking the springs on our vehicle of expression. If all the writing we do in life were some formal game, like the one we have for so long taught in school, the emphasis on higher-level diction might make sense. But students graduate from high school and from college unprepared for their writing challenges in life. *This is the shameful failure of our education system.*

My mother grew up on a Kentucky farm and had only

three years of schooling as a child. But she still went to college and wrote powerfully as an adult. It's possible many of us, today, would have become better writers as adults if our writing instruction had ended after the third grade, before the ways of formal writing were introduced.

Formal writing is something we may never need in real life. I can think of no good reason to communicate in such stodgy diction. Instead, let college students learn the nuances of writing for science in the Science Department and writing for history in the History Department, and so on for each major field, combining those nuances with Standard American English.

In the English department, we need to devote much of our time to introducing Heartspeak to replace the stinky hand-me-down writing methods our students were taught. *Mine is not a lone voice.* Other writers see the problem, too. Lewis Lapham writing on "The Pleasures of Reading," in *Harper's* magazine, May, 1975, says, "I have found that few writers learn to speak in the human voice, that most of them make use of alien codes (academic, political, literary, bureaucratic, technical)." If academic writers will write like we talk, giving up their fondness for the pomposity of "alien codes," their writing will find appreciative readers.

Chapter Five

Storytelling or Explanation?

"No, no! The adventures first, explanations take such a dreadful time."–Alice, from the pen of Lewis Carroll

Throughout my years of teaching writing in college, I have found few students, if any, who understand the difference between writing a story and writing an explanation. When I ask students to write a true story from their lives, most try to write an explanation of past events, instead. So I tell them, "A story happens at a specific point in time and place. Characters do and say things we refer to with *past tense verbs*. Details and dialogue are important. And the writer needs to help the reader 'see' what happened through the writer's eyes."

This definition of "story" seems clear enough, but it may take weeks of writing practice before students drop old habits of explaining things and fully enter into the process of storytelling. A few never succeed in making the switch, since year after year of writing instruction in school has implied, if not insisted on, this commandment: "Thou shalt offer explanations (not stories) about what others think, say, or do as you write for school." But, by stifling our first-person storytelling instincts, schooling ignores the opportunity to offer students powerful experiences of self-expression.

When talking to our friends, we tell stories. If we substitute explanation for storytelling when writing for school, we invite awkwardness, weakening our writing. Explanation is from the head. I'm not saying we should completely avoid writing explanation (also referred to as "exposition"). Combining exposition and story is what I am doing here and what students can do in almost any expository assignment (with the teacher's permission).

However, when teaching storytelling through personal narrative, it is important to help students understand how, if we have a point to make, story can illustrate the point better than explanation. Stories *show* by helping readers "see" in their mind's eye what is happening. Explanations try to make their point by a less powerful route.

This is similar to the difference a person can experience who has never seen an apple, being *given one to eat*, instead of just looking at a photograph of an apple. In the following examples of explanation compared to storytelling, we see explanation becomes *unnecessary* when the same thing is revealed in story. And stories are more powerful.

~~~~

Explanation 1: *Since I never liked school, it seems ironic I am a teacher, now, myself.*

Story 1: *I hated school as a child, feeling lost, alone, and bored. It seemed a teacher's job to torture children through year after year of boredom. And my teachers gave low grades I had to take home to Mom and Dad. I endured by telling myself, "When I am sixteen, I will quit school." But my days of misery in school became the path to my destiny, prompting the desire to bring change, to help others discover the source of powerful writing.*

~~~~

Explanation 2: *I like to eat a hearty meal in the morning.*
Story 2: *This morning at 6:30, I enjoyed coffee with ham, biscuits, and gravy at the local diner.*

~~~~

Explanation 3: *Some things become clearer for me as I write. They include. . .*
Story 3: *By pausing to look at my life, I realized . . .*

~~~~

Some readers may react to these examples, thinking, "I like both, the explanation *and* the story." But trust me on this. When teaching Heartspeak, if we don't insist students stay in storytelling mode, they won't learn to write powerful narratives. They will revert to the well-worn groove of explanation. So a focus on learning the difference in story and explanation is an absolute of teaching powerful writing. We need to set aside explanation for a while to become powerful storytellers.

One or two lines of explanation may be permissible in closing remarks of narrative essays — but nowhere else. And the explanatory way of initiating concluding remarks, using "In conclusion" or similar lead-ins, are no-nos. The temptation to give advice in a conclusion should be resisted, as well. Instead, we can *tell our reader what we intend to do*. This *implies* what we might advise.

Still, the most powerful way to end narrative essays is with story. The first line of the narrative may be dialogue — and the last line can be, too. We can close the door to our narrative in the same way we opened it. It enhances the feeling of "closure" by reminding a reader of the thoughts expressed as we began.

After mastering Heartspeak in personal narratives, students can combine personal anecdotes with exposition. I encourage them to do so as they write what I refer to as our "celebration of life research paper." In it, they are encouraged to celebrate their passion for a topic close to their heart as they write a persuasive paper researching it.

"Surprise Me" and "Stay off the Seesaw!"

Good writing will surprise, too. In other words, it's newsworthy. "I got up this morning and ate cornflakes," is not the sort of thing we tell friends, is it? It's a "So what?" remark.

We tell friends something more newsworthy, like, "When I got up, I discovered my roommate had eaten all the jelly-filled donuts. Then I remembered the cream-filled ones I hid in my drawer." This has the element of surprise.

Even when students succeed at writing strong storytelling sentences, they sometimes follow each sentence with another — an unnecessary explanation saying much the same thing. Many student essays take this "seesaw" approach, going back and forth with one sentence of story followed by another of explanation, reiterating what the story sentence says.

Years ago, I read a long student essay written with the seesaw approach. After I marked through all the explanatory sentences, the student revised his document and what remained was wonderful! I remember his writing so well due to its uncommon length and the unnecessary way *every* storytelling sentence was paired with another sentence *explaining* the same thing. When he removed the explanatory elements, it was half as long and many more times improved.

Avoid the Temptation to Start Stories with Explanations
To counteract students' tendency to write explanation in the first paragraph of a narrative essay, I recommend beginning with dialogue — what someone in the story said. This breaks the habit of using non-specifics and explanations.

Consider the following contrast in first lines.

~~~~

Explanation 4: *Everyone has a food he or she doesn't like.*
(Avoid starting essays with generalities like this.)

Story 4: *Yesterday, I told my neighbor, "If I must choose one food – and only one – to live on, it would be persimmons – ripe persimmons, that is. And my least favorite food is a greasy hamburger."*

~~~~

To write stories, we need to examine each sentence to see if it meets the criteria of telling what happened at one point in time and place, using simple past tense verbs. Here's another example of unnecessary explanation as seen in the first line of a student essay, followed by an example of how to start the same essay with dialogue.

~~~~

Explanation 5: *Writing has always been difficult for me.*
("Always" does not refer to one point in time and "has been" is not a simple past tense verb. So this is explanation.)

Story 5: *"Jason, your essay is full of grammatical errors," Mrs. Honeycutt said.* (This sentence includes dialogue and detail and tells of someone saying something in the past with "said," a simple past tense verb. So this is a story. It gains the sympathy of the reader who begins to identify with Jason's pain.)

~~~~

When we talk to family and friends, we tell stories of the events of our day. After so many years in school marching to a different writing tune, students believe writing for college needs to be a demonstration of explanatory intellect. They imagine stories are relegated to childhood, not welcome in college. They confuse explanation with story. See the examples below.

~~~~

Explanation 6: *John often rides his bike to the fairgrounds.* (This does not happen at a specific time in the past. It *explains* John rides to the fairgrounds *often,* using a present tense verb, "rides." The shift may seem slight, but if contrasted with the *past tense* version, below, we can see the first attempt is the stuff explanations are made of.)

Story 6: *Yesterday, John rode his bike to the fairgrounds.* (This example happens at a specific time and place and tells of a person doing something by using the past tense verb, "rode.")

~~~~

When I say, "Write a story," students try to follow my how-to's for story writing and may succeed in one essay. But they may revert to old habits in the next. Why is it such a big deal they not do this? It is essential to learn storytelling skills, since all writing can be improved (for any genre) *when we write like we talk, tell a story, and remove every unnecessary word*. It is no exaggeration when I say, "This is the foundation of good writing."

The Harsh Sound of Explanation

Explanation has a different sound. It is characterized by harsher, more didactic words. A common example in student writing is the word "that."

I ask students to remove "that" from their writing, since it is usually a throw-away word, easy to discard. In most cases, they can remove "that" without making other changes to compensate. But, when writing explanation as I am doing here, "that" is needed more often. Still, writers can eliminate many instances of it in explanation, too.

Depending on context, we can replace "that" with softer sounding words like "the," "this," or "who." They are softer sounding due to not having the "hard" ending—"t." Other hard endings include "p," "k," and "ch." Soft word endings promote a smoother "flow" in sentences.

The Rewards of Resisting Inertia and
Forming New Habits

We have a search tool at our disposal in word processing programs. Sadly, some students will not discipline themselves to do a proper search for what I call "no-no words" in their essays—words I list for them in our "Heartspeak Writing Checklist." Even after I take off points for the no-no words in their writing, some students still resist taking a few minutes for the search and edit process.

By their third narrative assignment, more students remember to search and edit. But those who continue to ignore the checklist do not get the best grades, since I take off points for each no-no word. Some of these words bring the harsh sound of explanation to stories. I don't enjoy taking points off, but it motivates students to appreciate the difference in edited writing like nothing else will do.

Students who want to improve their writing soon realize the changes I ask for in editing stories can be applied when editing all prose. Even research papers can be improved by minimizing the explanatory tone and adding stories as examples of the points the writer makes.

The Research Paper

When students write their research paper, I explain our semester's writing was meant to prepare them for this "grand finale." They should write it the same way they wrote their story-based essays, except it will include more explanation, quotations from research, and requires citing sources in the text and in the bibliography in the style their major field prefers. The writing will combine story and exposition, more like a feature article is written in journalism. But, when my students begin writing the research paper, some habitually return to their old methods of stinky formal writing.

I'm not convinced the research paper assignment is useful for most students. If they wrote one while in high school, they may still come to college confused about how to proceed with college research papers. And few will need to write them after their days in college.

But a required feature of the Junior English college class I teach is the research paper. So, after giving them several chances to write narrative essays by Heartspeak guidelines, I ask students to apply the same methods to writing their research paper.

To aid a student's transition from story-based essays to the required persuasive research paper, I help them choose a topic they care about. The passion they bring to writing a celebration of life research paper reveals and celebrates the writer's heart, even if the tone of the writing does not seem celebratory.

Any reader of a research paper is likely to wonder, "Why does the writer care about this topic?" So students are asked to tell a brief story as they begin the paper, to reveal why the topic is important to them. And their stories draw readers in like little else will do. Then they need to continue by braiding anecdotes, exposition, and research together, writing like we talk and removing every unnecessary word.

When I challenge students to find a topic they have a passion for, many tell me, "I can't think of anything I have a passion for." This is partly due to so many years of writing *for the teacher*, rather than students discovering their own reasons for writing.

The level of diction I recommend is not what students may think a research paper is supposed be. But this is an opportunity to bring a more conversational cadence to the writing. Of course, students need to fulfill other instructors' guidelines when writing for those classes. But many instructors will be open to students using the "Heartspeak" approach. Students should ask. In doing so, they will become part of the change needed in making Heartspeak the preferred method — the accepted norm — for college writing.

Due to not carefully reading my helpful tips and instructions for the research paper (where I say they should continue writing in first person as they offer story-based examples), some students begin using the stinky pronoun "one," rather than "I." Some return to using "big" words and long sentences. For those students, the research paper project is more of a chore than a celebration. But those who resist the old ways and write from the heart succeed in celebrating their passion.

Ancient Advice for Writing Research Papers

Cicero, in *Of Oratory*, refers to a quotation from Crassus. It offers the best short explanation I've found for how to write a persuasive speech. But the same advice applies to a persuasive research paper. Crassus says, "I had also been taught that, before speaking on the issue, we must first secure the goodwill of our audience, that next we must state our case. Afterwards we define the dispute. Then we establish our own allegations. Subsequently we disprove those of the other side, and in concluding remarks we expand and reinforce all that was in our favor, while we weaken and demolish whatever supports our opponents."

Beginning the research paper by offering a story revealing why the topic is important to the writer is an excellent way to secure what Crassus calls, "the goodwill of our audience." The trend among public speakers is to begin with a humorous story. And that's a good technique, too. But the introductory story should allow the reader to see the writer's heart as it pertains to the research topic. Just as happens in other narrative-based writing, the reader begins to identify with the writer.

When I say, "Tell a brief story as you begin," some students will write a long story on page one, then offer page after page of research and explanation. Instead, they need to braid story and research—like braiding hair—and like I am doing in writing this book. Explanations, stories from my life, and quotations are braided throughout. When students succeed in celebrating their passion, the result is powerful.

(See the sample research paper in the "Appendix.")

Chapter Six

A Minimum Security Prison?

School is a twelve-year jail sentence where bad habits are the only curriculum truly learned. I teach school and win awards doing it. I should know. —John Taylor Gatto

"Gather 'round, children. I want to show you how to make a 'Jack-o-Lantern,'" my kindergarten teacher said the Friday before Halloween. We watched in silent fascination as she cut open and cleaned out the big pumpkin before carving its distinctive scary face.

I have other great memories of kindergarten—with its short days offering life lessons through play. I remember making a tiny four-wheeled cart from a large match box and making a doll's cradle from an oatmeal box. We made construction paper chains to decorate the Christmas tree. And each little girl decorated a big, paper, dry cleaner's garment bag to create a "dress" and then decorated a paper-plate "hat" with tissue-paper flowers, before dressing up to march in the Easter Parade. Mom took a photo of me in my paper dress and hat.

But I was miserable in my other years of elementary and secondary education. My report card was never spectacular. All students hope to get the highest marks on their report. Then, year after year, most receive this message from their grades, "You're still not good enough." If a sibling gets better marks, parents may compare, saying, "Why can't you do like your brother (or sister)?"

I recall one of my sons having a close friend whose mother insisted her son get all "A's" in elementary school. If he didn't, she beat him unmercifully. He was an only child and was smart, no slacker. But, if he had even one "B," in the midst of otherwise all "A's," he still received a harsh beating.

A student shared the following story in one of my Freshman English classes. She said her younger brother, five or six years old, was fond of knocking on neighbors' doors, just to stand and talk. But his mom thought he was bothering the neighbors. So, to discourage him, she told the boy, "When we are born, we are only given a certain number of words. If we use them up too fast, we can't talk anymore." Of course, the class laughed. But it was a cruel thing for a parent to say. The little brother was given his first taste of the fear of speaking from the heart.

Children's souls are sometimes referred to as *tabulae rasae*—or "blank slates." Parents should speak the truth in love, rather than arousing the fear-monster. And teachers need to do the same, remembering what it was like to be a child. Antoine de Saint Exupery observes, "All grown-ups were once children, though few of them remember it."

School should be a safe space for children, whatever their age. Instead, trauma comes by bullying from other students. And, even though most teachers are dedicated and love students, some are hateful and do not have the temperament for teaching. Some are even sexual predators. We need a better way to discover rogue instructors and protect students.

I remember the day an African-American student in one of my Freshman English classes told the class about a trauma he experienced in school. He said, "A teacher told me I would never amount to anything."

I replied, "Such teachers do not belong in the classroom."

The young man often came to my office to discuss how to improve his writing. One time, he wanted help editing a letter he wrote to the editor of *EBONY* magazine, telling her what an inspiration she had been in his life. At the end of the semester, he slid under my office door a beautiful greeting card with a poem describing how teachers make a difference in their students' lives. I framed it.

A few years later, I saw this same unforgettable young man honored by being asked to give the Baccalaureate Address when he graduated. Of course, when I saw the boy who "would never amount to anything" given one of the university's highest honors, it brought tears to my eyes. Thinking about it, now, it still does.

The Power of Choice

The main way we can make school less like a minimum security prison is to give students more choices. More than producing insipid writing, the greater tragedy of the traditional approach to education is students are conditioned to always submit to some authority's opinion.

Certainly, children (and adults) need to respect their teachers. But when children begin thinking they must wait for an adult to tell them exactly what to do, their inclinations toward creativity or leadership, or developing the ability to say "no" to an adult who might intend them harm, is undermined. We need to balance respect for authority with respect for students, giving them numerous opportunities to make their own bold choices. We can guide children towards making courageous choices, if we are not habitually limiting their opportunities to do so.

Britannica Online defines "choice" this way: "in philosophy, a corollary of the proposition of free will – i.e., the ability voluntarily to decide to perform one of several possible acts or to avoid action entirely. An ethical choice involves ascribing qualities such as right or wrong, good or bad, better or worse to alternatives."

John Taylor Gatto, in his essay, "Against School," says, "We could encourage the best qualities of youthfulness — curiosity, adventure, resilience, the capacity for surprising insight simply by being more flexible about time, texts, and tests, by introducing kids to truly competent adults, and by giving each student what autonomy he or she needs in order to take a risk every now and then."

The Need for Adventure

Adventure accompanies any challenge, to some degree. And students hunger for adventure to dispel boredom. One entry defining "adventure" at *Dictionary.com* says, "a bold, usually risky undertaking; hazardous action of uncertain outcome."

When creating opportunities for adventure in the classroom, it becomes a teacher's responsibility to determine how much risk of hazard is appropriate for the sake of adventure. Adventure may involve risks on several levels, such as emotional risks (embarrassment) and physical risks (students getting hurt on a field trip).

Yet the risks involved can bring rewards for students. Sometimes, when children are encouraged to take risks, it is the result of playing a simple game. Relay races are an example. With such games, the challenge, the exercise, the break from sit-down instruction are among the rewards, whether or not accompanied by winning.

The Adventure of Choosing a Topic

Giving students choices adds an element of adventure to their school day, such as the adventure of embarking on a new writing challenge. Students need to discover a topic they care about to succeed in writing from the heart. But most of their lives in school, young people are given few choices. They are assigned to write about what others have written, what others have thought, what others have done—all chosen by the teacher. It can feel like an imprisonment of the mind. And, after so many years of this, students arrive in college unaware if they have any strong area of interest they might want to write about.

After I give the first assignment (where I usually ask students for the story of their writing history) my college students choose their own narrative essay topics the rest of the semester. Unaccustomed as they are to such freedom of choice, it soon becomes one of the things they like most about my class. But they sometimes encounter a mental brick wall when considering their choice of a research paper topic.

Most students dread the research paper. This is when their years of instruction in stinky writing can raise its ugly head, again, even if my students were writing powerful narratives to this point. They need to choose a topic they have an interest in—perhaps one relating to their major. But their writing succeeds or fails based on genuine curiosity—the writer's desire to know about the chosen topic. Often, students struggle making this choice. Perhaps Albert Einstein diagnosed the source of the problem when he said, "It is a miracle that curiosity survives formal education."

Years of classes offering few to no choices can make students think their interests don't matter in school. And being denied opportunities to pursue those interests results in a mental malaise that permeates education at every level.

I tell students the Heartspeak they used for narrative essays was preparation for writing the research paper. Their desire to know more generates the passion needed for what I call a "celebration of life research paper." Writing about our interests *from the heart* makes it a celebration. And writing "like we talk" avoids pomposity and awkwardness.

Still, some will assume the research paper requires traditional stinky writing. They return to writing in a language William E. Coles, Jr., says (in *The Play of Language)*, "was invented by English teachers for use in English classrooms, only." He adds this language is "as calculatedly dissociated from the concerns of the user and the world he lives in as it has been possible to make it." But students who continue writing from the heart avoid this pitfall. They can do this if they choose a topic they are passionate about.

We Learn Best What We Teach Ourselves

The two missing motivators during our youthful days in school are *choice and desire*. Children in America's schools are essentially following orders. They have few choices offered them, but having choices nourishes desire. Offering students freedom of choice is a form of respect—as well as good teaching.

The attraction for all of us in self-taught hobbies, sports, and more contemplative activities (like reading) has much to do with desire and choice. Throughout history, the greatest achievements have come from self-educated men and women. Isaac Asimov says, "Self-education is, I firmly believe, the only kind of education there is."

"What Do You Want to Do?"

I attended a Kentucky Philosopher's Association meeting years ago, and one of the speakers was a professor who explained how, on the first day of each new semester, he says to college students, "What do you want to do?" This was his mantra, a challenge issued whenever choices needed to be made—always shifting the responsibility for the direction of the class to students.

I wanted to try doing the same thing. I regret I never did. I teach online classes, now. But I wish I had tried it in a face-to-face classroom where students could bounce ideas off each other as they explored the rare opportunity for self-directed learning.

Teaching Myself

As a wee child, we are naturally inquisitive. We explore everything in our environment. We are self-directed learners. But our days in school seem designed to produce boredom, by offering little opportunity for self-initiated learning.

Education as we know it incarcerates young minds and bodies, then force-feeds them when they are not hungry. As a result, they come to dislike the taste of learning. But self-initiated, playful learning should counteract this, solving most problems in education.

Some students search for better tasting fare beyond the schoolroom. The inquisitive spirit a hobbyist exhibits allows her (or him) to learn more and faster, due to desire and passion. For instance, a cousin of mine loved to take apart old TVs and radios. By age ten or twelve, he was an electronics expert, due to his desire to know what made things work.

I loved reading and learning on my own as a child. I joined a travel book club, an astronomy book club, a cookbook club, a children's classics book club, and others. And I saved articles from Louisville's huge Sunday newspaper, keeping my files in a cardboard box on the floor of my closet. Freedom of choice fostered the desire to explore new worlds.

Since geography was my favorite subject, I read

encyclopedias, read books about world travelers, and sent off requests to travel agencies for brochures. I was the ultimate "armchair traveler."

At age fourteen, I persuaded my parents to purchase a 35mm camera, and I studied a mail-order photography course. My dream was to travel the world as a *National Geographic* photographer.

Then I Quit School

As early as age ten, while being forced to sit in school day after day in bored misery, I began jotting down my thoughts on what was wrong with school and how common sense could improve it. I didn't show these notes to anyone. I guess they gave me temporary comfort in the midst of my boredom and school-centered traumas. But here I am, today, writing on the same topic — hoping to make a difference.

When I complained about school to my parents, Mom said, "You have to go to school until you are sixteen. It's the law." But I knew what happened in school was a waste of time. I knew I could accomplish much more on my own. Sitting bored and frustrated in school, I said to myself, "It does not have to be like this!" I said it over and over. But I suffered in silence until the day I turned sixteen.

I sat in class counting the days. Then, February of 1962, I walked into the school counselor's office and said, "I'm quitting school." I began studying on my own the next day. . . *hungry to learn* whatever I could.

Few people heard of "home-schooling" in those days. Still, after a few days of studying on my own at home, I thought it odd when my parents—who insisted schooling was so important—took me away from my studies. Dad took me to work with him. He owned a one-man church furniture manufacturing business and had several apartment buildings. So he found plenty for me to do, painting window frames, cleaning apartments, or catching the oak pew ends coming out of the planer.

I didn't mind hard work. Working with Dad was a time of learning, too. I enjoyed spending time with him. I recall looking forward to our lunch together after a morning of working hard. Mom prepared two sandwiches for us to share, Spam and mustard on whole wheat bread, with two apples, all packed in an old bread wrapper. The fragrance of sandwiches and apples blended wonderfully, somehow, by lunch time. It tasted so good with a tall glass of water.

But, frustrated by being denied the hours to study at home, I returned to high school the next year, repeated the tenth grade, and graduated two years later. In retrospect, I see this was my destiny. It allowed me to see the problems with the way writing and other subjects are taught—at all levels of education — and conduct my own search for solutions.

Grading's Long-lasting Harm

When children must win the teacher's approval by getting a good grade, their view of their own abilities can suffer from years of being told through grading, "You need to improve. You are not good enough." Too often, they develop an "I can't do this" view of their abilities, likely to become a self-fulfilling prophecy. I believe this is why some students come to my college class writing at a low level of expertise. And they show, by half-heartedly following instructions, they believe they cannot improve. So they don't try.

I know my students can do it, if they give Heartspeak a chance. But it can be hard to convince them they have talent after years of being told by the grades they received that they are under-achievers. Does the child fail — or is it the education system relying on unrestrained tradition that fails?

Abolitionist Frederick Douglas writes, "It is easier to build strong children than to repair broken men." But the grading process in our schools might be regarded as twelve years of child abuse, producing broken spirits.

Why not make progress reports story-based, with a brief discussion of areas of weakness mixed with praise for a child's strengths? Some schools do this. It has greater promise for encouraging improvement than letter grades.

Criticizing Can Wait

Let's not criticize the writing of our elementary and middle school students. Why not just give them participation points for completing their writing project by the guidelines of the assignment? Why undermine a child's joy in the creative process? Why introduce fear of the teacher's disapproval? Instead, let fun fuel the writing fire within.

Writing games inspire improvement. Like playing the outdoor sports children love so much, *when they practice (writing or any skill), and if it is fun, improvement will come.* Combine this with praising what is good and students find more encouragement than if we criticize their errors.

The Learning Styles We Ignore

Teachers need to allow children with different maturity levels and learning styles the varying time frames they require to learn. But typical teaching methods allow all students in a class the same limited time for learning. Certainly, if a child cannot learn in the way we teach, we need to teach in a way the child can learn.

Malala Yousafzai reminds us, "One book, one pen, one child, and one teacher can change the world." The child who learns slower has no less potential for being a world-changer. Those children who "fall between the cracks" are the school system's failure. But the student who is left behind is treated as though it is his or her failure.

A different but equally harmful effect is experienced by the child who has "a gift" for learning a given task. This child can lose interest and motivation while waiting for other students to catch up. I know a seventeen-year-old who has been assessed as perhaps the smartest student in his school, but he hates school and completes his work only under duress. His schooling has not offered him the stimulation or challenge he needs.

The Workbook Approach — with No Child Left Behind
We have a way to help students achieve learning goals on their natural timetable — whether slow or accelerated. *It is self-paced workbooks.* It is hard for me to believe educators have ignored this sensible approach for so long. The traditional approach punishes slower learners and speedy learners, alike. The speedy ones are bored if they finish their work quickly and are ready to move on.

Since children learn a task or body of information at different speeds, many homeschoolers use the workbook approach. It can work well in public schools, too. The one year I kept my three sons at home for home-schooling we used workbooks. Each son worked at his own learning pace. When the check-up at the end of a chapter revealed he understood the material, he went on to the next challenge, learning something new. This non-threatening, non-competitive way of learning allows a child gifted in a certain area of study to learn at an accelerated speed, going far beyond others of the same age or grade level. But, with workbooks, those who need more time can achieve the same goals, without feeling left behind or lost in a classroom where a child's frustrations are multiplied by a failing grade.

Math? Oh My!

When I was young, I had a harder time learning math skills than some of my peers. Those who got good grades (meaning they could comprehend new material on the schedule set by the teacher) went on to the next assignment, leaving "slower learners" (like me) behind.

When I became confused in my algebra class, I gave up. The pace of assignments required me to understand more quickly than I could, even though I wanted very much to learn to play the algebra game. What seemed like fun for one week soon left me sitting in silent misery, while other students were moving on. Is my experience an exception? No, and I think it is the reason many students fail. They are simply left behind.

I was in my algebra class the day President John F. Kennedy was assassinated. The principal made the awful announcement over the loud speaker. And I have other sad memories of that class. The teacher had mental problems. He was fragile. Some students taunted him, getting him off-track and frustrated, until little was accomplished on those days. I saw the teacher's pain and the students' cruel mischief.

Soon, I couldn't tolerate the situation any longer, so I went to the school counselor and discussed it with her. She listened quietly—but I could tell by her response nothing would be done about it.

Lawmakers, Do No Harm

Lawmakers are prone to make laws our teachers have little opportunity to influence. Those laws, such as the Kentucky Educational Reform Act (KERA) passed in 1990, (the one many college students tell me made them hate writing) must be carried out by the lone teacher standing before a classroom of children, even if he or she quietly disagrees with the whole idea. KERA was unpopular with teachers and students, alike.

Over my many years teaching college students who graduated from Kentucky high schools, I recall only one telling me she *enjoyed* writing for KERA. I asked students about it each semester when I taught in face-to-face classrooms. Most said KERA made them hate writing. Is this the outcome lawmakers envisioned? If students hate writing, how can we expect them to do it—or become powerful writers? KERA had good intentions, but when it became clear it was doing more harm than good, not putting a speedy end to it allowed it to become legislated child abuse for untold numbers of students.

One of my students shared an interesting story. She said her writing for KERA received the highest scores possible and was selected as a sample for other students, statewide. But, when she went to college, she was perplexed when her writing for a Freshman English class received low marks. This is less likely to happen if elementary through high school students have the same Heartspeak agenda presented to them as I recommend for college. Then their education could be marked by continuity, rather than confusion.

Why So Much Trauma?

When I ask college students to write stories of their own history as writers, trauma is usually part of their story. In addition to nation-wide teaching skewed to testing, other traumas occur. Teachers assign write-offs for punishment. Students tell me when they had to write anywhere from 25 to 100 times, "I will (or will not) blah, blah, blah," it did permanent damage to their desire to write. Or if a child in elementary school completes an assigned writing, enjoys the assignment, and thinks of it as a masterpiece, only to receive the criticism of a teacher, the disappointment can turn the child against writing, too.

So I indict, along with the traditional way writing is

taught, individual traumas children experience in school as a second cause why so many lose their potentially powerful writing voice. Add to this the boredom and frustration associated with spending so much of our lives in what seems akin to a minimum security prison, and we have the opportunity for daily misery for children and their teachers.

What other choice do parents have? Parents can begin asking for change—for schooling to offer less judgment and more learning games. Another option some families choose is home schooling.

At the end of this book, I share a research paper from one of my students telling of his experiences in home schooling. It is no accident his is one of the best research papers I've received. His intellect is one factor—but his love of learning developed through the home schooling adventure is another.

A good friend of mine is raising her granddaughters, and she encourages them to enter academic competitions. Her girls attend public school. But she insists, "It is the home-schoolers who take most of the top awards in academic competitions." Of course, not every parent can or will choose home schooling. So, for the sake of all the children in our schools, the changes I'm discussing here are long overdue.

One More Thing Is Needful

To succeed at teaching well, a teacher should love teaching and love students. I know teachers who have a doctoral degree or a master's degree, but they will never be "master teachers." *They don't like people* and leave a trail of trauma in their wake. They should choose a different profession.

Trauma teaching tactics include the obvious—coming to class intoxicated, cussing, sexual harassment, rudeness, and having "teacher's pets." Teachers sometimes embarrass students, insult students, label students, refuse to help students, lecture over the head of students, and assign an unreasonably heavy work load. The problem becomes outrageous if such a teacher is tenured and no one puts a stop to these behaviors. It's not hard to identify them. Many of their students drop the class. When I had teachers like this, I was the first to drop.

When I returned to college as a student, after a twenty-year hiatus, I heard stories of teachers who should not be in the classroom. One of them taught at the small extended campus I attended. The odd thing was how much abuse his students tolerated before anyone told on him. I learned (after the fact) he came to class drunk, insulted students, and, when one girl got up to leave his classroom in tears, he hollered, "Sit back down!" She did. Students didn't alert the administration until he just stopped showing up for class.

At the same extended campus, I took a class from a morose fellow who seemed annoyed to be teaching the six students who signed up for his class. Each student was asked to prepare a presentation. When I began giving my talk, he soon stopped me, not allowing me to finish what I prepared. Another student said, "I was enjoying her presentation." But the instructor would not allow me to continue. I'm convinced he did it because he disagreed with the points I made.

In *Integrated Learning Through Story*, Carol Lauritzen and Michael Jaeger describe the sort of teacher who inspires students. "Our friend made a lasting impression on us when he said: 'I teach who I am, not what I know.' . . . By these meaningful words our eyes were opened to see teachers as influential human beings rather than simply holders of certificates, licenses, lettered degrees or titles."

Chapter Seven

When Writing Is Fun, Improvement Will Follow

The creation of something new is not accomplished by the intellect but by the play instinct acting from inner necessity. —Carl Jung

Children need play and adventure woven into the classroom experience. If this is missing, they are bored most of their young life in school. But boredom is no stranger to college classes, either—and for the same reasons. In *Control Theory in the Classroom*, William Glasser observes, a "good comedian is always a good teacher." Of course, teachers have a wide variety of personalities, and stand-up comedy is not a required course for teachers. But any teacher can create a lighthearted atmosphere in the classroom, at least some of the time. I've seen in my own teaching how a "spoonful" of laughter can help the lesson go down.

Let Us Play!

Robert K. Johnston writes, "Involving not only the body but the emotions and mind, play affords at least a momentary integration of life." Whether we are three years old or ninety-three, one of the things we all need in order to be sane and happy is to take time to play and, at times, we need a friend to share the joy with.

As a child, my joy was diminished when playing alone.

Ideally, in school we find play friends in our classmates and teachers. Life not accompanied by laughter is foreign to childhood.

I agree with W. H. Auden, when he writes:

Among those whom I like,

I can find no common denominator.

But among those whom I love, I can:

All of them make me laugh.

One of my favorite movies is *Conrack*, starring Jon Voight, Paul Winfield, Madge Sinclair, and Hume Cronyn. Based on a true story, it shows how a new teacher helps the profoundly under-educated children in a one-room school benefit from his playful way of teaching. It is a classic story, illustrating the divide between hard-nosed traditional teaching methods (as seen in two people: the school's principal and the superintendent) and the more playful, loving approach of the new teacher. Laughter is no stranger in his classroom — and neither is the love between teacher and students.

A major symptom of mental illness, according to psychiatrists, is the loss of a sense of humor and the ability to play. Donald Winnicott writes, "Psychological healing is bringing the patient from a state of not being able to play into a state of being able to play."

Play has been denigrated, held in low esteem, and

sometimes forbidden in the academic setting. In or out of school, the phrase "He (or she) is just playing," suggests a lack of appropriate seriousness. This may be one reason educators sometimes think a rigorous approach to learning—with an overdose of homework, memorization, the threat of tests—is necessary. What this means for students, though, is stress, fear, failure, and a loss of Heartspeak. Rather than using fear as the basic motivator, let's replace fear with the anticipation of the joy of play.

In her January 26, 2015, article in *The Atlantic* (online), titled, "Joy: A Subject School Lacks," developmental psychologist Susan Engel writes, "You can force a child to stay in his or her seat, fill out a worksheet, or practice division. But you can't force a person to think carefully, enjoy books, digest complex information, or develop a taste for learning. To make that happen, you have to help the child find pleasure in learning—to see school as a source of joy."

Our Grand Experiment

I passed out the syllabus for my two Freshman English classes on the first day of the spring 2000 semester. Perhaps the dire predictions for the new millennium were in my thoughts as I contemplated what it might be like if a class of 20-plus students entered into an experiment based on the premise, "We are the last people on Earth. It is up to us to save what we can remember of human history and culture."

I introduced myself to my new students and explained, "This semester, I want us to imagine our planet experienced a catastrophe and only those in our classroom survived. All the schools, museums, libraries, electronic devices, and art works were destroyed. Every home was lost—along with private collections of memorabilia, books, films—everything. So it becomes our task to recall and record whatever information we can about history, language, game playing, musical notation, constructing and playing instruments, all arts and crafts. We need to share our combined wisdom on child-rearing and relationship skills, first aid, how to build homes and furniture, and much more."

I continued, "For each class session, I want everyone to write about a historical event or cultural artifact relying only on memory—even if it is incomplete. It might be Mother Goose rhymes, the Declaration of Independence, song lyrics, Bible verses, or how-to instructions for your favorite recipe. The possibilities are endless." Then I added, "And I will trust you to not look to the Internet or any other source for the items you bring to class. What you write must come from memory." Each time we gathered, students settled down in our circle of desks to read aloud what they wrote.

One time, the class was surprised when one young man

brought a long passage from Shakespeare, and proved he had *not* consulted a "source" by reciting the lines from memory. Another time, a girl who admired Theodore Roosevelt's daughter, Alice Lee Roosevelt, shared what she learned from years of reading about Alice Lee, who was her mother's namesake.

The class became a treasure hunt into the terrain of our souls. And it was empowering for students to consider what they knew but took for granted, since their previous days in school focused on what they *didn't* know.

At the end of the semester, each student brought copies of the daily contributions he or she had made. They walked our circle of desks, placing copies on each one. In this way, we collated and created a huge book, titled, *Culture as We Remember It*. The university print shop bound the books for us. At the final class session, students went home with their own copy. I cherish mine.

I tried the experiment just one semester. But I will never forget it. One of my colleagues told me a young man from my class worked with him each day after my class. More than once, the student told the professor what an amazing experience our class had been that day. It's a good day in a college classroom when students remain awake—even more so when they can describe the experience as "amazing."

Play and Consequences

Pretending we were the only survivors of a catastrophe was a game we played for our grand experiment. James P. Carse writes in *Finite and Infinite Games*, "To be playful is not to be trivial or frivolous, or to act as though nothing of consequence will happen. On the contrary, when we are playful with each other we relate as free persons, and the relationship is open to surprise; everything that happens is of consequence. It is, in fact, seriousness that closes itself to consequence, for seriousness is a dread of the unpredictable outcome of open possibility."

Play is essential to writing well, since playfulness and creativity are the same thing. Unfortunately, the notion is prevalent in education that learning need not be fun. But we learn best when at play. Too often, adults who have forgotten how to play try to take control of a child's or an adult's learning, converting it to a serious experience with serious methods.

A teacher cannot force a student to have fun, laugh, or play. However, if the teacher makes an opportunity for play and enters into the spirit of play herself, it is likely to be contagious. Few things are more contagious than yawns and laughter, and maybe the first is so prevalent in the classroom due to a deficit of the latter. I cherish memories of the playfulness of some of my own teachers. They became my role models. When the teacher joins in the fun, the fire of learning burns brightest.

Playful Teachers

I have heard it said, "We learn best while laughing." If so, teachers who avoid using humor in the classroom lose a valuable pedagogical tool. In *The Joy of Not Knowing It All: Profiting from Creativity at Work or Play*, Ernie J. Zelinski explains, "Experts in creativity have observed that solutions are often triggered by humor. Seriousness hurts the creative flow."

Zelinsky refers to a study done among high school students where two groups were tested for creativity. "Two equal sub-groups were formed. One of the sub-groups enjoyed the half-hour before the test by listening to a recording of a comedian. The other sub-group spent the half-hour in silence. When subjected to the test, the students in the first group did much better than the students in the second group."

When I think back over comments students made in my classes, the funny quips and stories are the ones I recall. I'll never forget the student who was in his dorm taking a shower when a fire alarm went off. He grabbed his toiletries and rushed outside, wrapped in a towel (but with his underwear in place). In order to not be late to my class, he decided to come as he was — towel-wrapped and toiletries in hand. Shocked and amused, I called the school newspaper. A photo of the student sitting at his desk wrapped in his towel appeared in their next edition.

My Funny Role Models

One time I engaged a colleague in a water gun fight in the halls of academia. He is legendary for his playfulness, taking comedy props with him to class, such as a set of scissor-action plastic hands he claps when he says something clever. His students love it. Just for fun, I wrote a lengthy poem about him, saying, in part,

> Our department's most outstanding feature
>
> Is an unassuming, humble English teacher.
>
> Perhaps he's less than a perfect bloke,
>
> But he has made my day with a well-told joke,
>
> And yards and yards of entertaining prattle.
>
> We even faced off in a water-gun battle.

This is not great poetry, but taking time to write silly poems often served as a refreshing play break in my long days of teaching face-to-face classes.

The best memories of my own teachers are linked to the funny things they said or did. One of my graduate level English professors had a tie tack that looked like a big, bright green spider. The day he wore it to class, students didn't notice, at first. He began his lecture. Then one girl saw the spider and screamed, thinking it was real. When our professor grinned, we realized the tie tack was an example of his wonderful, twisted sense of humor.

Another time, the same professor was sitting in class when we arrived. He was dressed in hippie garb, instead of his distinguished "uniform": light blue shirt, necktie, and slacks. We thought we had a visitor. None of us recognized him. Colleagues he passed in the hall didn't recognize him, either. It was remarkable the way it took longer than the big green spider incident for us to realize what was happening. The element of surprise—like humor—makes such events memorable.

It is commonplace for English teachers to enjoy language play, even those who do not bring a playful spirit to the classroom. But teachers *and* students benefit from the positive atmosphere of a classroom filled with grins and laughter.

Arnold Toynbee writes, "The supreme accomplishment is to blur the line between work and play." If we fail to give our students opportunities to play, we limit their creativity and lose the aid to memory humor can offer. A playful teacher will set the mood, creating an irresistible atmosphere of play.

Modeling a Playful Spirit

When I taught in face-to-face college classrooms, students loved it when I was playful. As the semester began, I sometimes sang the "Homer Simpson Drinking Song," to the tune of "Do, Re, Mi" from *The Sound of Music*. (Homer's version can be found online.)

I don't drink alcoholic beverages, myself. I don't like them. But my college students loved it when I sang Homer's song. It begins, "Dough, the stuff that buys my beer — Ray the guy who sells me beer." Parodies are a classic writing game.

I recall other attempts at playfulness in other classrooms. Sometimes, I wore a pink or blue wig. Or I introduced the lesson for the day by rapping, with a battery-powered microphone adding drum rolls and other sounds. Another way I tried starting the class with a grin was to ask a different student each day to read something funny to the class from an old book called, *Humorous Primary Recitations*. These childish gems remind us we're all still children, at heart. Here's an example.

Magic Words

My grandma knows the magic words

That open up the gate

That leads into that wondrous land

Where elves and fairies wait

To come back to this earth again,

Where once they lived in rhyme.

My grandma says these magic words

Are, "Once upon a time."

Now, I try to maintain a playful spirit in the announcements I post for online students. I'm sure my online humor generates groans, but students say they appreciate the upbeat posts. One time my boss asked, "What is it you're doing that brings such enthusiastic evaluations?" The answer is simple. I try to create the sort of class I'd want to be a student in.

A Strangely Difficult Assignment

If I give students an assignment asking them to write about the funniest thing that ever happened to them, they write it, but many say, afterwards, "This was the hardest paper I've ever tried to write. I couldn't think of anything really funny." While writing their story, they think, "Surely, there's another story—the truly funniest thing that happened to me—but I can't recall it." It's an interesting phenomenon.

The difficulty we have remembering and writing our funny life events may be due to so many years of trying to write formal English. It rarely connects to playfulness. A serious tone shuts the door to our playful side, until, even when we needn't be so serious while writing, it can be hard to think funny.

When young students do not enjoy writing, they do their assignment to get the adults around them to quit their nagging. But without a real desire for their task, they may not learn from it. Children benefit from a play-based approach to writing — or any academic challenge. And adults do, too. Teachers have endless possibilities for playful writing assignments if our goal is to let freedom — and laughter — ring.

"Do It Good or Not at All?"

This reminds me of a story one of my grown sons told me, recently. His playful approach to writing a high school assignment made him famous — at least for one day. He said his English teacher always asked the students to summarize the points of their essays in a final paragraph. So, one day when my son forgot to do his homework, he arrived at class, and a friend reminded him the assignment was due.

My son pulled out a piece of paper and wrote his name at the top. Then he wrote a summary at the bottom of the page, saying, "If I can't do it right, I just don't do it at all." His teacher got a big laugh from it and read it to the class. He even read it to his other classes that day — and gave the "essay" a "C."

Teachers and students, alike, benefit from humor in the classroom. But at least teachers get paid to be there. The greater loss in a humorless classroom is the student's opportunity for mental and emotional growth by what might otherwise be a relief from boredom and an invitation to creative playfulness.

Language Play ~ Even in Textbooks?

Teachers can introduce the guidelines for a writing game and maybe share examples from their own writing, or from previous students, or from some great writer in history. Even parodies of the works of great writers can be useful. Reading the parodies can serve as a back door introduction to the classic works of literature — and to the way we pay homage to the originals by writing parodies.

We need to let children (and adults) play at writing, enjoying the challenge and the fun. Teachers can model their own enjoyment of writing by playing with language and sharing the results with students.

I remember what fun it was when I first read *Harvard Lampoon* parodies. My favorite was *Bored of the Rings*, a parody of *Lord of the Rings*. And much of the humor in *Mad* magazine relies on parody, as well. How wonderful it would be if students found their textbooks even half as entertaining.

Why not bring more humor and playfulness to the writing and illustrating of children's (and adults') textbooks? This can easily be done by including stories and cartoons. Story-based writing is — like humor and surprise — an aid to memory.

I read with delight the humor included in *Writers Inc.*, a textbook by Patrick Sebanek, Verne Meyer, and Dave Kemper. It has a chapter on writing research papers where it features a half-page drama titled, "You Ain't Nothing but a Hound Dog." In it, the teacher, Mrs. Marmalade, has a writing conference with a student named "Elvis." She looks at his first attempt at writing a research paper and offers advice. Then Elvis asks her, "Will you take a peek at my new song?"

Mrs. Marmalade replies, "I would be delighted. Hm. Very good. However, 'ain't' is not proper diction and 'ain't nothin' is a double negative. This is a charming little tune, Elvis, but, as you see, it needs some editing. A correct title would be 'You Are Nothing But a Bassett Hound.'"

A humorous reading I used in the college classroom on occasion comes from *Falstaff*, by Robert Nye. It is his chapter titled, "The art of farting." Yes, it's crude, but farting has been the occasion for laughter since we were toddlers. And Nye's piece brings guffaws in the classroom. Nye's character even illustrates the sounds farts make with diagrams of his and his friends' farts. It is funny in many ways, not the least of which is the idea of making a "serious" study of farting. Starting a class discussion with humor helps keep students awake.

Writing Games ~ the Classics

Since "game" can be defined as "any rule-governed activity limited by time and space," the list is endless. And, as class assignments, some writing games are always "winners."

I think first of "interviewing an older family member." Parents or grandparents are the obvious choice. And the interview can be a memorable experience for both the younger interviewer and the elder storyteller. In *Your Personal Mythology*, Sam Keen reminds us, "Strange as it may seem, self-knowledge begins with self-revelation. We don't know who we are until we hear ourselves speaking the drama of our lives to someone we trust to listen with an open mind and heart."

My college students often write wonderful character studies about grandparents. And the character study is a cousin of the interview. Both assignments are great writing games. One thing I ask college students to do is include in their narrative some of the stories the parent or grandparent tells. An alternate assignment is asking students to write narrative essays about the most memorable storyteller in their life.

Certainly, these interview games (the character study and the memorable storyteller), can result in preserving much valuable family history that otherwise might be lost. Don't we wish we had interviews with all our ancestors? In *The Simple Life*, Charles Wagner reminds us, "And the very base of family feeling is respect for the past; for the best possessions of a family are its common memories."

Sometimes a college instructor will ask students to interview the person in the next seat on the first day of a new semester—and then they go up to the front of the room and introduce each other to the class, a great way to break the ice.

Another excellent assignment is the "rewrite game." When playing this one, the student needs to write a short story (maybe 150 to 250 words) in "like we talk" style. Then, the instructor will ask for one or more rewrites of the same story, so the student can appreciate the difference in a variety of writing styles.

The second version might imitate super-pompous higher-level diction. The third version may be a drama—just dialogue. Another version may convert the story to a poem. And the student might rewrite it as a news report, journalistic style. We find no end to the possibilities. Artistic students may want to illustrate their work or do one rewrite as an artistic interpretation.

Indeed, I think it would be great to start every school year (or semester) asking students to write a story, and then each week rewrite it another way, throughout the duration of the class, in addition to regular writing assignments.

Literature classes ask students to read examples of powerful narrative writing by well-known authors. But when asked to *write about those examples,* students are *not* encouraged to offer their narrative of *the experience of reading the selection.* Formal analysis is the order of the day. But narrative can incorporate analysis, too, or vice versa.

The one semester I taught "Introduction to Literature," I asked students to *tell the story* of the family tree of one great work of literature. I wanted them to become detectives, finding the many spin-offs that happen over time when a piece of literature is imitated. Parodies and movie versions were two of the many possibilities. This assignment helped students appreciate the significance one piece of writing can have over the centuries — the way it continues to inspire and influence creativity.

Let the Writing Games Begin!

I visualize a learning community where children are told, "Writing is a game." A teacher might introduce the *Yesterday Game* (a journal), or the *Haiku Poem Game,* and the *Create a Skit for Three People Game* (to act out for the class).

One of my favorite writing games is the *Alliteration Game.* In one version, each student writes a sentence where most words begin with the same letter of the alphabet. The sentence might have a theme, such as food. For the letter "M," a student could write, "Macho Mark munched on macaroni."

Another version of the alliteration game tells a coherent story, start to finish, where most words begin with the same letter. Again, it needn't be strictly alliterative, since it will have conjunction junctions and other words necessary to connect the alliteration, grammatically. I recall an alliterative story I read as a teenager, titled, "Prodigal Son in the Key of F." It begins, "Feeling footloose and frisky, a featherbrained fellow forced his father to fork over his farthings" as it retells the Bible story of the Prodigal Son. (The full version can be found online.)

In writing, as in any other game, desire, enthusiasm, and practice are the keys to success. If we decide to make a career of writing, then a greater commitment is required. Until then, let kids (and adults) in school write for the fun of it! If they love to draw, we can encourage them to illustrate their writing. If they love music, we can encourage them to make a song of their poem.

One way to include a variety of learning styles is to ask students to combine visual arts with writing. One time I asked college students to write and illustrate a true event from their lives as a colorful cartoon strip. So I created an example.

In my cartoon, based on a true story, one of my grown

sons was at a bar with a friend. One said, "Where are all the women, tonight?" The other said, "It's Wednesday night. They must be in church." So the two drunks drove to church, where they sat in the audience acting obnoxious, as drunks will do. Then, at the altar call, one of them tearfully ended up "getting saved."

Every teacher's commission should be, "First, do no harm—to a child's love of learning." Teaching writing as a game can help avoid the stress students sometimes experience when writing for school. And it can do the same for the fun-loving teacher who sets the tone for the class.

If students have fun and if writing is not something they dread, I'm convinced they will become strong writers before they are of high school age, just by writing for the fun of it, Heartspeak style. When they arrive at high school, they will not be suffering anxiety and confusion over writing. By playing with words, without fearing a teacher's red pen, skills and creativity can blossom. Students should come to school each day, enthused, asking, "What game will we play, today?"

We sometimes think, "If it's easy, and if it's fun, it's not sufficient for accomplishing serious goals." But play has been unduly maligned as insignificant—just a diversion. Instead, a playful spirit is the key to creativity and to an abundant life. As adults, we need to take frequent play breaks to preserve our health and sanity. But children *play* to grow, to learn, to survive. When we side-track them away from play to traditional pedagogy, we do not take advantage of the way they learn. While play does not guarantee powerful writing, powerful writing is rarely produced without it.

Examples to Inspire

A language game even college students enjoy involves writing playful stories in mock Shakespearean English. I wrote the following paragraph for a Freshman English class to introduce "Ye Olde Assignment," before I asked students to write a page of playful banter in a similar style.

> Once upon a time on College Hill, a score of lively souls joined head and heart to a worthy task — to tell a tale of their days questing for truth and romance (whichever cometh first). The lords and ladies put their quills first to ink and then to parchment to tell a tale of four-score words and ten. With long suffering and vain oaths didst they labor by the candle's glow. Some drank a hearty brew to engender a happy heart. Thence the scribes didst make merry as they fancied the reveries of lords and ladies long dead, all the while inscribing such words as none considered might ever come from his or her pen. Verily, methinks it a memorable eve when the archaic tales were told on College Hill.

The semester I gave this assignment, we had been studying Mark Twain's *Connecticut Yankee in King Arthur's Court.* We ended the study with a "Lords' and Ladies'" banquet where students dressed up like nobility from the Middle Ages.

For any language game, it's a good idea to have samples for students to look at to get the idea. A good example of writing about the importance of *place* in autobiographical narrative comes from N. Scott Momaday's, *The Way to Rainy Mountain,* where he writes:

> Rainy Mountain is in Oklahoma; it is a sacred place to my people. My father says, looking across that landscape makes him feel that is where Creation began. He returned to grandmother Aho's grave in the summer after she died. She had lived her long life in the shadow of Rainy Mountain and, even though my father calls another place home, he—and through him—I too have lived in the shadow of Rainy Mountain. There was something in grandmother an 'ancient awe' that she passed on to my father and to me. It is a relic in this modern world—but a priceless treasure to me.

Momaday's writing about a special place might be used as an example if an assignment asks students, "Where are you rooted in terms of place?" Students can describe the place and tell the stories of events associated with it. Eudora Welty observes, "A sense of place has been important in my own writing and in my life. It helps to provide continuity and explain the way events turn out in human relationships."

My life, too, is tied to a special place. The sixty-one acres of south-central Kentucky woods where I live became my home through a series of events suggesting it was my destiny. It was originally owned by my great-great-great-grandfather, Allen Hunter, who married Rhoda Anderson in 1806 Virginia. But my place is the only remnant of his land still owned by a descendant. The old family stories associated with it are fascinating. I love this land and hope my descendants will cherish it, too.

I invite my reader to contrast my explanatory paragraph (above) about my home place with Momaday's storytelling paragraph about Rainy Mountain. Mine lacks any reference to what a character said. And his is more powerful by having more details, more discussion of the family's historical attachment to the land, and more of narrative's simple past tense verbs. The people he writes about are seen through the eyes of his heart. Perhaps storytelling comes easily to him since Momaday comes from a long tradition of native American campfire storytelling.

Chapter Eight

In the Beginning Was the Word, the Story, and the Campfire

The real art that dealt with life directly was that of the first men who told their stories round the savage campfire.
— Robert Louis Stevenson

"In the beginning was the word," is as true in our daily life as it is an archaic sense. Even in the womb, we hear our mother's words. So it is appropriate to refer to our first language as our "Mother tongue."

Speaking fluidly is an ability most of us take for granted. We assume powerful speech is a birthright. But, if a child is denied the opportunity to hear language in the first few years of life, the challenges this child will face are profound. In the documented reports of feral children, we are told they never learn to speak, other than a few words. Learning language early is essential to the full development of their mind, heart, and personality.

Feral children suffer language deprivation. But the uncountable masses of American children taught to write according to traditional methods is tragic, too. The good news is that we can abandon the traditional methods and put more sensible writing instruction into place. We have a remedy.

Stinky writing is reversible. We can undo much of the harm caused by teaching traditional style writing and turn things around — one person at a time (after the fact, at any grade level). We also need a nation-wide revamping of teaching writing from the first grade onward.

From Speaking to Writing

The terms we use referring to writing are often the same ones we use referring to speech. We "say" something when we write. A writer "speaks" to us. But with the way writing has traditionally been taught, the powerful way our words can affect a listener when we speak tend to get lost when we begin to write — since we are told in school *not* to write like we talk.

We begin learning to write by going off to school at age five or six. So how do the excited, noisy, happy first-graders of America get turned into such voiceless under-achievers in their native language by the time they graduate high school? Their writing suffers a disconnect from the heart when schooling begins emphasizing writing from the head.

The capstone of such schooling seems to be the dreaded high school research paper. One of my three sons was told he would not be allowed to graduate high school without it. He finally got it done — and never looked back. He has had no need for those "skills" in the many years since.

Instead of writing research, papers, students need to be sure to have strong computer skills. My college students sometimes can't even copy/paste. Most employers are not going to care if they can write a research paper. Many *will* want students to be able to navigate a computer.

In *Searching Writing*, Ken Macrorie says, "The 'research paper' has become an exercise in badly done bibliography, often an introduction to the art of plagiarism, and a triumph of meaninglessness—for both the writer and reader." Even though college students are asked to write a research paper in high school and in some of their college classes, most of them still cannot write a good research paper when they arrive in my Junior English class. So the high school research paper writing experience had little benefit. And it taught more of *what not to do* than what to do—since it is the pre-eminent "stinky writing" project of their years in school.

The Scholar's Quest

Many Amish folk live in my community, and I sometimes hire them for odd jobs. My Amish neighbor was doing some remodeling for me when he posed this question. "How many scholars do you have in your classes?"

The word "scholars" gave me pause. It was not one I used much when referring to students. So it caught me by surprise. But it also gave me a longing to see students return to thinking of themselves more as "scholars" than the party animals many have become. Their social life can cause dozing students in college classrooms in the mornings. When I taught in face-to-face classrooms, I found evening classes were different. Students were awake and ready to start partying as soon as their evening classes ended. Not all students fit this mold, of course. But many do.

To be scholars, college students need to approach their classes as though on a grand quest. The quest begins with a "question," a genuine desire to know about something related to the subject being taught. This way, their time in class needn't feel like a waste, no matter how disinterested they may be in the subject to begin with.

Even if the instructor does not assign a paper to write, a student can conduct an inquiry into an interesting aspect of the subject. This may result in enjoying a class he/she initially had little interest in. Success in learning is often a piggyback affair, joining our own interests to what we study in school.

The Campfire Experience

Marni Gillard writes in her book *Storyteller Storyteacher*, "The practice of hurrying children away from talk and into work with paper and pencil—of discounting their oracy—has grave effects on their literacy." Gillard's observation reminds me of my own elementary school report cards saying, "Talks too much." I remember trying hard to stop—but, soon, I heard my teacher's voice calling my name, again, saying, "Stop talking!" Children have a need to talk during the school day, more than in the few minutes over a hurried lunch. A good way to meet this need is the "Campfire Circle" where children can tell stories from life. The classrooms of today are not amenable to fires and toasting marshmallows, but when children (or college students) know a time is set aside for moving their desks into a circle and telling real or imagined stories, some of the original "campfire experience" can be duplicated.

In *Orality and Literacy: The Technologizing of the Word*, Walter J. Ong explains, "The spoken word forms human beings into close-knit groups. When a speaker is addressing an audience, the members of an audience normally become a unity, with themselves and with the speaker. If the speaker asks the audience to read a handout provided for them, as each reader enters into his own private reading world, the unity of the audience is shattered, to be reestablished only when oral speech begins again. *Writing and print isolate*."

In *Dreamquest*, Morton Kelsey reminds us of another dimension where the power of words is diminished. He says, "Something is lost when a story is read aloud, rather than told; it no longer seems to spring from the depths of the soul." Nevertheless, today, whether reading them aloud or sharing personal stories impromptu, we have fewer opportunities for telling our stories face-to-face in a group than was common in cultures of the past.

The Chinese say, "Let us draw closer to the fire, so we may see what we are saying." What is it our culture has lost by replacing the glow of the campfire with the glow of the TV, smart phone, and computer screen? TV watchers are passive recipients of entertainment. By telling our stories face to face, around a real or imagined campfire, we share our hearts.

The loss of a campfire storytelling experience could be another reason so few people are powerful writers. Shouldn't powerful communication be a natural ability flourishing from childhood? American society today offers few opportunities for face-to-face community storytelling. One notable exception is Alcoholics Anonymous (AA) meetings where participants are encouraged to share their stories over a cup of coffee.

For those who have never been to open (or closed) AA meetings, I can verify from experience, they are powerful. One semester, I invited an AA speaker to share his story with my college students. Students listened, fascinated. We could have heard a pin drop in the classroom. The lessons learned from hearing first-person storytelling of life experiences can be powerful.

The AA experience offers something our culture has almost lost—the opportunity to tell our story to a community we feel a part of. Barry Lopez speaks of our need for it in *Crow and Weasel* when he writes, "The stories people tell have a way of taking care of them. If stories come to you . . . learn to give them away where they are needed. Sometimes a person needs a story more than food to stay alive."

I became aware of the strong storytelling tradition of tribal cultures years ago through reading *I Have Spoken*, a collection of native American speeches written down by Army secretaries at the scene of historical encounters between Indians and blue-suited representatives of the American government. I read those speeches with an ever-increasing sense of awe inspired by the eloquence of their profound words. And I wondered, "What is it about tribal culture that produces such powerful words?" The children who sit around their campfires grow up with the same powerful storytelling skills.

Now I know the answer to my question. In her book, *Sending My Heart Back Across the Years: Tradition and Innovation in Native American Autobiography*, Hertha Wong quotes a native American storyteller saying, "I am sending my heart back across the years." Stories in the campfire tradition come from the heart, the same sort of Heartspeak students can write and share in our classrooms, today.

To test my theory in face-to-face classrooms, I began offering students a campfire experience by asking them at one class meeting to write a personal essay they could read aloud for our next class session. When they returned for the next class, we moved our desks into a circle and they read their essays aloud, receiving encouragement and feedback from their peers. Afterwards, at a third class meeting I asked students to write a paragraph letting me know how they felt about sharing their stories with the class. Here are snippets from a few of their replies.

One girl wrote, "After Tuesday, I feel like I know some of the people in here. The father's touching account of his son's birth, the hilarious story about the kid who got a ticket for speeding in his friend's car, and my personal favorite — the woman and her sick kitten gave me personal glimpses into the souls of people I would have otherwise never known anything about."

Everyone had positive comments. Here are six more.

~~~~

"It creates much more discussion in the class than any other class presentation."

"I think if we could read all our papers aloud before grading, we could get helpful feedback."

"By everyone reading aloud, I could compare my work to the work of my peers."

"I heard some great stories that brought out ideas of my own."

"I think once we get back to regular class time, there will be more involvement. More people will say what they think."

"I really, really liked our first storytelling class period. The atmosphere was very freeing. Thank you for allowing us to do this."

~~~~

The tradition of imitating the storytelling of our elders has almost disappeared. In oral storytelling traditions, frequent storytelling produces enthusiastic, powerful speech that might be easily converted to powerful writing. Shouldn't such storytelling flourish from childhood?

The classroom "campfire" creates a psychic space, not a physical place. Marilou Awiakta refers to such experiences as being in "primal space," saying, "The longer we stay in primal space, the more jarring it is to return to what many American Indians call, 'the other world'—a world not of poetry but of lists." Can we visit primal space once more and recover our powerful voice? Our classroom campfire says we can.

Chapter Nine

Avoiding Common Errors

Writing is easy. All you have to do is cross out the wrong words.
--Mark Twain

To Learn a Subject Teach It

What about teachers who themselves have little idea what powerful writing is about? It took me years to learn what, now, at age 70, I consider only a modicum of knowledge about good writing. I discovered the bad — and the good — on my own, a little here, a little there. Each semester while reading student papers, I still find "bad stuff" students do that I need to stop doing, myself.

It's easier to see an error in someone else's writing. So I add each discovery to our class writing checklist. First, I teach *myself.* Then I offer the same tip to students. "If you want to learn something well, teach it to others" is sound advice.

Writing first person narratives is the foundation of good writing. But writing them is just step one. Our stories are not "finished" until the writer removes every unnecessary word in the editing stage. Doing so, the sentences may become a little less like we talk. Still, a conversational sound should remain the goal. So it is important writers read their writing aloud while editing to discover when they are not writing like we talk.

The writing checklist for my classes offers other tips on improving writing. I want to share, here, a discussion of a few of the most common writing errors discussed in the checklist.

Begin Early ~ Revise Often

Students are sometimes tempted to write their essays an hour or so before they are due. This is a mistake. I tell students to revise each essay at least three times (ideally, once a day over three days) before posting it for me to grade. We see our writing through new eyes after 24 hours and find additional ways to improve by letting a document rest overnight. For instance, I edited the pages of this book so many times I've lost count. Students needn't assume the pristine copy of their writing is perfect, either. Edit, edit, and edit again.

Avoid "So What" Sentences

Many student writers begin their narrative essays by explaining what people in general do at some non-specific point over time. Often, such sentences speak of what is common knowledge. I call these "so-what sentences." We need to state specifics, instead — something newsworthy. And it should refer to the actions of a specific person, at a specific time and place with past tense verbs.

Sometimes the whole first paragraph a student writes is a "so what" paragraph. When editing, the writer should remove it. When I read a student's document, I often add this note: "Just go ahead and remove the first paragraph and begin with paragraph two. It's where the story begins."

Here's an example of sentences students tend to write in the first paragraph—and then need to remove while editing. "Almost everyone has heard of video games. In the past 20 years they've become a booming industry." This introduction is common knowledge and explanation. Neither contribute to powerful narrative essays.

Instead, the story writer might begin an essay on video games this way. "Last night, in my dorm room, I spent eight hours playing *World of Warcraft*." This makes reference to time, place, the main character, and specific details told with a past tense verb, "spent."

Eliminate Doubling

The goal of removing unnecessary words can fail due to old habits we don't realize are "unnecessary." When writing under a teacher's assigned length—whether of pages or number of words—students sometimes develop habits of using word pairs—and they don't always correct this when editing their stories for my class. These doubling habits are kinfolk of clichés (trite, overused phrases).

Doubles may have two verbs, such as "He hurried and ran," but one is sufficient. Adjectives, nouns, and other words can be doubled, unnecessarily, too. I call it, "The doubles game," but *it is not the sort of game we should play when writing.*

Recently, I read a student paper with ten "doubles" in it: "taught and lived," "came and asked," "born and raised," "seen and treated," "power and responsibility," "beliefs and choices," "input and suggestions," "wisdom and instincts," "hours and hours," "children and childhood." A common double is "If we pause and think about it . . .," and it should be edited to say, "If we think about it." Choose the best word and toss the other one.

A Simple Way to Avoid Run-ons and Comma Splices

"Independent clause" is another term for "sentence." "Independent" means it makes a point and can stand alone as a sentence. Dependent clauses are sentence fragments we sometimes use to add details to independent clauses.

I recommend having only one independent clause per sentence, since doing so gives each point more emphasis. This means we should avoid joining *two independent clauses* with a coordinating conjunction. These conjunctions are "for," "and," "nor," "but," "or," "yet," "so." But, occasionally, for variety, joining two independent clauses in one sentence is okay.

Having one independent clause (making one point per sentence) helps us avoid run-ons and comma-splices. And it tends to improve writing in other ways, too. We can still add detail with *dependent clauses,* if needed. So some sentences may still be lengthy, even if they have only one *independent* clause.

One point per sentence aids a reader's comprehension and provides emphasis by creating a mental breathing space between the points we make. We need to *avoid semi-colons* for the same reason. I find no good reason to mash one sentence up against another with a semi-colon. When our writing has mental "breathing space," readers are not as likely to miss important points.

If we write several short sentences, one after the other, it can seem choppy. To offset this, we can add a coordinating conjunction *as the first word* of the third or fourth sentence in a paragraph. This maintains conversational sound and flow while preventing choppiness.

Don't Let the Squiggles Get You!

My student writing checklist rarely discusses spelling, punctuation, or grammar. But by giving attention to the warning indicators—usually red, blue, or green underline squiggles provided by their word processing programs—students should correct those errors, too. It is important to remember some of these indicators show up only after we place the ending punctuation for a sentence. So students need to re-read and correct the full document, giving special attention to the squiggles.

Short Paragraphs

My writing demonstrates my practice of breaking paragraphs, frequently. This enhances a reader's comprehension and pleasure while reading. I suggest breaking when a point seems completed and the focus shifts. Sometimes students give me papers with page-length paragraphs. *This is not acceptable.* We need frequent paragraph breaks. Paragraphs need at least three sentences. Up to four or five sentences before providing closure is fine, too. (But, in this discussion of errors to avoid, my paragraphs tend to grow longer than that.)

Avoid "Groupspeak"

Of course, students should be asked to avoid slang, profanity, and cliché's. But those no-nos are acceptable in a story's dialogue where cussing should be represented by a combination of letters and nonsense keyboard characters.

Students sometimes ask, "Why not use clichés?"

My answer: "Using clichés (except in writing dialogue) takes the writer to a different (undesirable) level of what I call "groupspeak," not "Heartspeak." And groupspeak is a groove we get into, inviting more of the same. Clichés are part of our conversational culture, but, as we write in first person, we can express what our heart wants to say better if we choose our own phrases. We are more likely to write from the heart in our *unique* voice, when we avoid clichés.

Verb Choices

The careful use of verbs involves important choices we make when writing stories. Storytelling needs to be done with *simple past tense verbs,* in most cases. The exception is if using past tense is confusing—maybe if the action takes place often, perhaps every day. Just make sure changing from past to present this way does not confuse the reader. The occasional present tense verb is okay—if the action spans past and present. Reading our writing aloud as we edit is the test for making such decisions. Make choices that will help readers not get confused.

Avoid "Has," "Had," "Have," and "Would" Verb Phrases and Use Simple Past Tense Verbs

The "has/had/have" verbs are often combined with other verbs to become verb phrases. Such verb phrases *need to be edited* to contain just one past tense verb. Students sometimes write a whole essay using has/had/have verb phrases. But this weakens the writing and is not concise. It adds a second word (or a third) when only one is needed. So change "had written" to "wrote" or "has been running" to "ran." Like other words we avoid, on occasion "has," "had," or "have" are necessary to prevent awkwardness or confusion. But it's rare.

Another non-specific way students refer to the past (instead of using a past tense verb) is "would." Sometimes, the first word I mark for removal is "would," since it is so common in students' first paragraphs. It is a fine verb to use in conversation. It is the way we talk, but it rarely refers to a specific point in time. So it weakens storytelling.

"Mom would bake chocolate cakes whenever anyone had a birthday," is typical of the way a student might use "would" in a verb phrase to refer to a non-specific point in time. Instead, the writer needs to use the simple past tense, saying, "Mom *baked* one of her amazing chocolate cakes for my birthday last week." This implies she bakes chocolate cakes for family events but uses the past tense verb "baked," rather than the explanatory verb phrase "would bake."

Also, like the "has/had/have" phrases, the danger in using "would" is writers who use it one time tend to continue using it sentence after sentence, paragraph after paragraph, rather than using a simple past tense verb. So avoid "would." It is not a bad word. But what student writers do with it often weakens their storytelling.

Avoid "Excited Present Tense" Storytelling
When students tell stories to their friends in conversation, they often use present tense, even though the event occurred in the past. This is similar to the way TV news programs refer to past events in present tense. It is a practice I disagree with, though, and likely to confuse.

Students sometimes are excited when they tell their friends stories of their adventures in present tense. (As in "Next, we go . . ." instead of "Next, we went . . .") So I call this "the excited present tense." *When writing personal narratives, tell the stories with past tense verbs, not the excited present tense.*

"Able to" Is Not Do-able

Avoid combining "able to" with other verbs.

Bad stuff: *I was able to get up at 6:00 a.m.*

Good stuff: *I got up at 6:00 a.m.*

Nix "There Is"

Remove "There is" (or "there are") as the first two words of a sentence. Instead, begin with the subject of the sentence or some sort of introductory phrase.

Bad stuff: *There are many reasons to take Ruth Rogers' English class.* (Explanation)

Good stuff: *Ruth Rogers' English class helped me understand how writing like we talk – from the heart – is the key to powerful writing.* (Story.)

To "Be" or Not

Some teachers insist students should avoid using "be verbs," such as "am," "is," "are," "was," and "were." But I don't agree, except when a "be verb" creates a verb phrase. "He was walking home from school," combines a past tense "be verb" (was) with a verbal form ending in "-ing" (walking).

In most cases, we should change the verb to, "He walked home from school." When context allows, use simple past tense, not "were going," but "went," not "was eating," but "ate," to be more concise and for more powerful storytelling.

You Dirty Dog, "YOU"

The pronouns "you," and "your" should be eliminated from personal narratives, unless they are found in dialogue. On a rare occasion, writers may need to use "you" to speak directly to the reader. But it's not good form to do so, *unless necessary.*

The common shift we make when speaking—changing from first person to the self-conscious (indefinite) "you"—should be edited out of our writing. Other teachers refer to this "you" form as "the generic you," or "the indefinite you," or "the indeterminate you," or "the impersonal you." I like to call it "the self-conscious you," since we often make this shift from "I" to "you" when we are thinking of ourselves and could continue telling our story in first person, saying, "I."

Often, the shift from "I" to the "self-conscious you" occurs when speaking of something we feel emotional about. We say "you," to distance ourselves from our emotions when we want to avoid tears and choking up. Doing this with "you" in writing diminishes the power of Heartspeak.

This evening I was watching *Genealogy Roadshow,* and a lady who was emotional about all she had learned about her ancestors said, "It makes *you* feel like crying." Of course, she was referring to herself. If she had said, "It makes *me* feel like crying," she might not have succeeded in holding back the tears. So she distanced herself from the emotion by using the "self-conscious you." We need to avoid this distance in writing. *Keep the emotion* by writing in first person.

Another acceptable substitute for the "self-conscious you" is "a person," or we can specify "students," "parents," or some other group the writer has in mind. I tell my students, *"Don't use 'you' in writing* – except in a story's dialogue." All is fair in dialogue—except profanity needs to be represented in nonsense symbols. Not to do so is a distraction to some readers. We need to maintain the goodwill of our audience.

"Better" Not

Avoid using "better" as a verb. Its most common use is as an adverb.

Bad stuff: *"I want to better my writing."*

Good stuff: *"I want to improve my writing."*

Breaking the Adverb Addiction

Stephen King, in his book, *On Writing: A Memoir of the Craft*, says of adverbs, "The road to hell is paved with adverbs." But in conversations, we use adverbs to add emphasis to our remarks, words like "really," "very," and "always." Those three are the most common and should be edited from our writing, except in dialogue (where we needn't change what a speaker said).

Most adverbs explain "how," "when," or "where." But in storytelling, we need to avoid explanation. If we have sufficient details, dialogue, and action in a story, explanation is unnecessary. Remove adverbs, unless doing so changes the basic message of a storytelling sentence or removes an important nuance in the message. Most adverbs are disposable, without making other changes to compensate.

The goal of editing our writing is to remove anything unnecessary and/or distracting from the flow and message of a sentence. But, if we decide we must have an adverb, we can maintain the "flow" and message of our sentence better if we position the adverb as the *first* or *last* word of the sentence.

Few, if any, adverbs should survive editing in stories. They convert a storytelling sentence to explanation. And, like all the skills we learn in storytelling, we should strive to use fewer adverbs in all our writing, not just in our stories.

"That"

The number one unnecessary "clutter" word students use is "that." It appears on occasion in this book, since I'm explaining things. But I strive to remove every instance of "that" I can—if doing so does not undermine the point.

By ending in "t," "that" falls into the category of words

with a harsh sound. They interfere with the flowing cadence of a sentence. Often, in storytelling more than in explanation, all instances of "that" can be removed — without making other changes or else by substituting another word.

Students are surprised how many instances of "that" they can remove without doing harm to their sentences. I received an anonymous student evaluation saying, "This class is all about the small things. Retrospectively, these small things really have improved my writing. I was looking back over a paper I presented this past semester, and all I saw were the (literally) hundreds of "that's" in the paper. It was like needles on a chalkboard. Ruth, thank you for the little things. Thank you for making my writing clearer. Thanks for helping me communicate my thoughts just a little bit better."

(I ask students to not refer to me as "Professor Rogers," but to feel free to refer to me as "Ruth," like the student did above. I don't use titles with my name.)

The Sound and Flow

The sound of writing like we talk is the foundation of good writing. Each word we use brings more than its dictionary definition. The sound carries baggage, too. We need to listen to the sound of our writing. Reading it aloud is the best way to accomplish this.

Some words are harsh. Some are softer and more fluid.

Some have three or four syllables, while another word meaning the same thing may have one syllable. For example, I use "often" (two syllables) instead of "usually" (four syllables). Avoiding words with harsh sounds and editing to be concise, using fewer words along with using words with fewer syllables, enhances the "flow" of our sentences. Flow promotes the reader's comprehension and pleasure.

Also, as we begin making a point (the message of the sentence) we should avoid interrupting it with clever repartee, adverbs, interjections, asides, or any unnecessary qualifier, such as some adjectives. When we let the message of a sentence *flow*, the reader's pleasure and comprehension increase. "Don't interrupt others is common courtesy. "Don't interrupt yourself" is good writing.

Does Our Writing Pass the Read Aloud Test?

When I taught in face-to-face classrooms, I introduced students to the powerful storytelling of Garrison Keillor by playing a recording from his radio program, *The Prairie Home Companion*. My students loved his humor and storytelling skill.

James J. Kirkpatrick's November 30, 1987, newspaper article, "Garrison Keillor's Writing Lessons," discusses the powerful examples Kirkpatrick finds in *Leaving Home*, a book of stories from Keillor's broadcasts. Kirkpatrick says of *Leaving*

Home, "Every writer who wants to master the gift of narrative can learn something from it." He identifies lesson one as, "How does this read aloud? If your piece of writing listens well—if the sentences flow smoothly through the ear—you can be certain the piece will read well."

Keillor's skill stands squarely on the "write like we talk" foundation, and may be the classic example. His humor is superb. Any student of writing can benefit from listening to Keillor's gift for storytelling, radio drama, and humor. Even though he is retired, his stories are available in recordings. If students want to polish storytelling, humor, and performing skills, *recording their own stories*—in audio or video—is a good way to start.

The Need for Variety of Sound

Often, good writers make the following choices to vary the sound in their sentences—maybe without being aware they know to do so. The skill is based on the need for variety.

1) Unless it is intentional (for effect or emphasis) it is better to not start several sentences in a row with the same word.

2) For variety, after using a noun or proper noun as the subject of a sentence, we need to use an appropriate pronoun for the next reference to the subject in the same or the following sentence in the

same paragraph.

3) We avoid the choppiness created by using numerous short sentences if we use a coordinating conjunction to *begin* our third or fourth sentence in a paragraph. And it maintains a conversational tone. (The coordinating conjunctions: "for," "and," "nor," "but," "or," "yet," "so." The acronym is FANBOYS.)

4) If we use a coordinating conjunction as the first word of a sentence, we need to avoid repeating it as the first word of another sentence in the same paragraph.

5) In general, we should avoid repeating a word or a "cousin" word based on the same root in the same sentence or in the following sentence. Example: *"The student studied all night"* has a subject and verb with the same root.

The Sound of Silence

Arthur Burt reminds us, "Nothing happens until the pain of staying the same outweighs the pain of change." Grading is one way teachers help students consider the "pain of staying the same." Due to confusion — and fear of grading — few of us escape anxiety about writing. This fear reveals itself through the all-too-common "writer's block" in college. I tell students, "Just go ahead and write *about* the writer's block, expressing your frustrations and anxieties over writing. This will enable you to lay it to rest and get beyond it to write about other concerns."

When I remind students, "Just stop doing the bad stuff and there's nothing left to do but the good stuff," my goal is to persuade them it is do-able. They *can be* powerful writers. So the "bad stuff — good stuff" message may sound negative, but it is a prelude to this more positive message, "Write from the heart, telling stories the way we talk" to achieve the goal of "Heartspeak."

I love it when students tell me my introductory remarks to the class inspired them to begin thinking, "Maybe I can discover what it means to be a powerful writer. Maybe it's not just a 'gift' for the chosen few."

Writing teachers sometimes refer to Standard American English as "the language of those who report the news each day." All of us who grew up in America should know what it sounds like, even if we grew up in a family speaking some variation of it. Our writing voice is acquired just by growing up in our native land.

Of course, some of the skills involved in good writing come only by reading the works of powerful writers. We gain an awareness of well-crafted sentences when we read great writing. But, even for students who are well-read, their writing can remain confused until they learn to "say" in writing what they might say when speaking.

Writing this, just now, I think, "Hmm. This sounds so reasonable, so self-evident. I wonder why it must be said, and, even with saying it, why most educators seem to ignore the results — the way so few of those who receive their education in America's schools enjoy writing." The profound influences from our past — tradition and trauma — can paralyze our writing voices. Most students graduate and then avoid writing. Writing anxiety produces more than bad writing. It produces *silence*.

Heartspeak

Does your heart beat fast?

Do you swallow hard?

Does something inside say,

"Don't go there. You're walking on hallowed ground"?

Then you're in the territory of powerful writing.

Go ahead.

Peel off a section of soul and plop it on paper.

–Ruth Rogers

Afterword

After at least twelve years of writing instruction in elementary and secondary school, if traditional methods worked, my students would not still be struggling to feel competent in writing. — Ruth Rogers

In "Open the Doors to Creativity," an article in the *Times Educational Supplement* of September, 1995, Valerie Thornton sympathizes with secondary school teachers, saying, "Teaching creative writing to secondary schoolchildren is often a more daunting prospect than giving them a lesson in report writing, interpretation or analysis. Additional skills are needed: skills that English teachers have had knocked out of them by the very education system that led them into teaching English. How many of us were encouraged to submit poetry or fiction as part (and a very small part, if that) of our training in English?"

Thornton could have added, "How many of us were encouraged to write personal narratives?"

Since it is true the teachers of our children may have little experience writing personal narratives, it follows they also are not likely to know how to teach it to their students. Our teachers need training in writing Heartspeak. When they put aside the traditional methods of teaching writing and embrace the power and promise of writing their own stories, the change we need will come. Powerful writing results from digging into the gold mine of our souls, telling stories that speak to the reader's heart. Whether teachers or students, we don't need to wait for a writing class to begin putting our stories on paper. Start now.

I'm not suggesting other teachers must teach as I do. But I hope a discussion will begin, resulting in needed changes in how we teach writing. The traditional way leaves most students afraid to write. We need to silence *the ugly fear-monster within* who whispers, "You'll never be a powerful writer." We can do this if we will shift our methods of *teaching writing and doing writing* from the head to the heart.

In this book, I visited the classrooms and concerns of my teaching life, hoping my reader will join me in asking for long overdue changes to how we teach writing. I invite lawmakers, teachers, administrators, counselors, parents, grandparents, students—and everyone else—to take up this task. We owe it to every child in school—now and forever—to replace our failed teaching methods with Heartspeak.

Think how great it would be if we could ask each teacher this question (from a poem by John Oxenham), "Where are you going Great-Heart, with your eager face and your firey grace?" And the answer would be, "I'm going to teach my next class."

Appendix

[Thanks to Will White for sharing his APA style research paper. References pages have been removed to discourage any temptation to plagiarize. —Ruth Rogers]

Homeschool: The Benefits to Students

Will White

Western Kentucky University

Abstract

This paper explores the benefits of homeschooling to students. It begins with the story of a homeschooler. The story shows the underlying power of the way he was educated and the benefits he has derived. Research is presented indicating the benefits or detriments homeschooling may have to students in general. This research supplements the story. First, the scholastic achievement of homeschoolers is shown. Second, extra-curricular activities are considered. Brief examples from the homeschooler's life are provided. Third, the issue of socialization is addressed. Finally, the moral or relational benefits of homeschooling are discussed.

Homeschool: The Benefits to Students

"When you're finished with that we'll go to town and get ice cream, since you got done early today." What ecstasy! Mom often said such things. She was good at creating incentive. It was an important skill as a homeschool mom. The 15 years she spent teaching me and my brother were marked by leniency, gentleness, and reward. But they instilled in us a great propensity for academic rigor and toil. I know no harder worker nor more reliable intellect than my brother Sam. Mom's love will benefit us for the rest of our lives.

I attended Bowling Green Christian Academy when I was six. I didn't love going to Kindergarten, and Mom and Dad were already homeschooling Sam. So I began homeschooling too. My family became my teachers, helpers, and guides. When I learned phonetics, pieces of paper were all over the wall for my aid. The vowels were stuck to the floor for me to walk on. I first understood addition when Sam explained it with marbles on the living room carpet. A homemade basketball goal from Dad was my reward for learning the times tables.

Mom and Dad selected and ordered curricula for us to use. Most of our books were from A Beka. They got us excited when the books came in the mail, and they let us open the boxes. I didn't see through this tactic until high school. Sometimes I disliked my books. Now I adore them. I love them for their clarity, quality, and sound Biblical teaching. The curricula came with quizzes, tests, and solutions. A 100% earned a trip to the treat basket!

Mom was our lesson planner and teacher. But Dad, the principal, was our English advisor, and band leader. My love of music began when he played his guitar and sang with us. We had a few good groups of friends. With the Robersons we met at the park and threw acorns while our moms talked.

The Geralds were our companions for many years. We

often went with our friends on homeschool field trips. These were organized by the Allen County homeschool group. We went to a milk bottling plant once. And we were given a tour of Kenney's Cheese. I loved visiting Domino's. They let each homeschooler make his own pizza! Good people and wholesome things to do were plentiful throughout my education.

Many good times were had with our friends at the Scottsville YMCA. Ryan, Amy, Amanda, Zac, Nat, Bradley, and Caleb all joined us there for PE classes. We loved playing soccer in the summer. Basketball was good, too. In later years we were on the swim team together. We passed time at practices and glorified games with absurd thoughts and foolish talk. But at every swim meet and gymnastics contest, my family awaited, cheering me on.

When we were older, we joined a homeschool co-op in Bowling Green, Kentucky. There Sam and I experienced a classroom setting. We also became part of a community of good people who are dear friends today. I played on the Barren River Homeschool Association basketball team, where I met some of the young men who are my closest brothers now. I spent high school in the uplifting company of like-minded peers and the trustworthy friendship of our loving parents.

When homeschool was done, I arrived at my public university to find I was different from my peers. Academically I was well prepared. Socially I was closer to my family and farther from popular culture than others. I attribute nothing bad and everything good to my education. Dad and Mom taught me to fear God and to trust Jesus for salvation. Their love for me is analogous to His. Nothing is more beneficial than these loves.

But what about other people? Is homeschool as beneficial for everyone as it was for me? First let's look at academics.

Scholastic Success

Education studies show high academic achievement in homeschoolers. Scholastic success of students who are homeschooled does not necessarily mean homeschooling benefits students' performance. But it is in favor of the idea.

In the spring of 1998, a study was conducted administering standardized tests to 20,760 homeschool students around the nation (Rudner, 1999, p.1). The author writes, "Home school student achievement test scores are exceptionally high. The median scores for every subtest at every grade (typically in the 70th to 80th percentile) are well above those of public and Catholic/Private school students." (Rudner, 1999, p.27). Rudner (1999) states of standardized test scores, "the median scores for home school students are well above their public/private school counterparts in every and in every grade," (p.16).

In 2008, a similar study collected standardized test scores and demographic information from 11,739 homeschoolers in all 50 states and two territories (Ray, 2010). This study also showed high achievement. Ray (2010) writes of his findings, "First, the overall scores are well above public school student averages. This is consistent with the body of extant research. It is not a surprise," (p. 22). The demographic breadth of this study was expected to reveal more moderate performance from homeschoolers than had been indicated before. The opposite was true. Homeschooler's scores were higher above public school averages than previous research showed. Ray (2010) writes, "Homeschool student achievement test scores are exceptionally high. The mean scores for every subtest (which are at least the 80th percentile) are well above those of public school students." The author concludes there may be a causal relationship between homeschool and high academic performance (Ray, 2010, p.23).

Many homeschoolers are concerned about college

admission. We consider it a test of our elementary and high school education. People are also fear an "informal" education will be a detriment to a student's future. Gary Mason, a college admissions professional who has frequently worked with homeschoolers, writes:

> Research showed that our homeschooled students had above average SAT and ACT scores (1210 and 29 respectively). They also performed better academically. They had a combined cumulative grade point average of 3.47, compared to the 2.91 shared by the general student population. (Mason, 2004, p.1)

Mason (2004) attributes homeschooler's college preparedness to their education background. He writes, "These students were well prepared for college by their homeschooling experience," (p.1).

Many college admissions officers view homeschoolers favorably. In a study by Jones and Gloeckner (2004) over 78%

of admissions officers interviewed expected homeschoolers to perform at least as well as other students in their first year of college. The majority of the participating institutions have an official homeschool admission policy (Jones & Gloeckner, 2004, p. 20).

I was well prepared for college. My homeschooled friends say the same. My brother received a 35 on the ACT. We and our friends have high academic standards compared to the people I know with other educational backgrounds. We don't all just happen to be smart. Our parents taught us to work hard. Doing poorly in school disappointed not a stranger or an enemy, but our loving mom and dad. School was family.

Our opportunities have not been limited. No abnormal difficulty accompanied my admittance to Western Kentucky University. Many of us have academic scholarships. My friend Kyle received an athletic scholarship. AP classes were not available to me, but many of my friends have taken dual credit classes. Several of us tested out of English 100 and 200.

But academics are only part of education. Athletics, travel, and practical experiences are important. Does limited extra-curricular opportunity constitute a detriment to students who homeschool?

Extra-curricular Activities

Simoncini and Caltabiono (2012) say for most children positive development results from consistent participation in extra-curricular activities, and research has shown benefits in adolescents as well. Plecnik (2007), points out homeschoolers often do not have access to the sports and activities offered to public school students. He claims homeschooled and private schooled students in North Carolina have a legal right to participate in public school programs (Plecnik, 2007, p. 10). But having a legal right doesn't make something convenient. Some homeschool friends of mine did play on a public school football team. But most of us never tried to get involved in any such thing.

For some, limited access to public school activities may be a detriment. For me, it was not. Many extra-curricular activities of our own and of our homeschool groups would have been impossible had we been in public or private school. I mentioned the YMCA sports my brother and I played as kids. They led to us organizing soccer games on our own with friends. Later, we and a group of guys from the Bowling Green homeschool group invented a game called jacobball. This rough and tumble sport is now enjoyed among the homeschoolers of the area. The BRHSA now has a track team, a baseball team, and a football team in addition to the good old Trailblazers basketball team.

Good non-school activities never lacked for me. Mom and Dad have paid for piano lessons with the goodhearted Mr. Leland Humphrey since I was a kid. I have developed a love for theater through many community shows and Arts Alive productions. Sam and I have had games to play, chores to do, or farm work to enjoy. We have struck up successful projects on our own, like our 16-foot-long medieval style trebuchet.

The best examples of my homeschool extra-curricular activities are our family road trips. We packed our school work into the GMC Suburban and struck off across the country. Sometimes it was just to visit family in Missouri, Florida, Mississippi or Texas. In the fall, we went along with Dad's family on pheasant hunting trips to South Dakota. Wherever we went, we stopped at national parks. I have visited at least 106 different national parks, sites or landmarks. And we read every sign.

Socialization

A frequently proposed detriment to homeschooling is poor socialization. People are afraid students won't develop proper social skills if they do not spend lots of time in school with other children. Research indicates otherwise. Medlin (2000) in his research review on the topic writes:

> Home-schooled children are taking part in the daily routines of their communities. They are certainly not isolated; in fact, they associate with — and feel close to — all sorts of people. Home schooling parents can take much of the credit for this. For, with their children's long-term social development in mind, they actively encourage their children to take advantage of social opportunities outside the family. Home-schooled children are acquiring the rules of behavior and systems of beliefs and attitudes they need. They have good self-esteem and are likely to display fewer behavior problems than do other children. They may be more socially mature and have better leadership skills than other children as well. And they appear to be

functioning effectively as members of adult society. (p. 119)

This conclusion agrees with my experiences.

We have been involved in church and homeschool communities since I was small. When I was in high school I enjoyed frequent social events in the homeschool group. Costume parties, movie viewings, Bible studies, and English country dances were regular affairs. I have spent more time with my family and less time with friends than the public schoolers I know. But I was never shut out from community. Few homeschoolers are.

I have known many homeschoolers, and I have heard many people talk about homeschooling. They say, "Homeschoolers are always so polite!" Maybe they just don't want to offend me. But it's true. The homeschoolers I have met tend to be kind, lucid, and friendly though sometimes reserved. They are often better equipped than their peers for conversation with adults.

My parents taught me how to speak correctly. They taught me how to be respectful and courteous. They let me spend time with good kids, so I could learn how to play with different people. The most important social qualities boil down to love. These were taught to me by my mom and dad. Some social skills are useful, and some are idiotic or bad. I sometimes call myself socially inept. I'm not on *Facebook,* and I don't know all the characters from *Parks and Recreation.* I am missing out on some useful things and lots of idiotic and bad things. Most of my homeschool friends are more socially apt than I. But they would agree. What's important they learned from their parents.

Of all the people I know, the homeschoolers are less likely to be socially maladjusted. The kids from broken families are not as likely to be homeschooled. I would take the loving influence of my parents over any level of social affluence or ability. Homeschooling is different from public schooling. But it doesn't detract from a student's socialization skills.

Last but not Least

The benefits leading parents to choose homeschooling are not just academics, home-grown extra-curricular activities, or outstanding politeness. Parents often choose to homeschool for religious or family reasons. They desire at least to protect their children from influences they consider harmful. Thomson and Jang (2016) write, "An implicit desire to limit exposure of teens to sex, drugs, violence, and negative peer pressure appears to motivate many parents to homeschool their children," (p. 283). Ray (2002) says, "Homeschoolers also want to retain the responsibility of raising their children and not have their children raised by strangers," (p. 50). The greatest benefit to a student who homeschools may be a relational or spiritual one.

I have said my parents taught me to trust in Jesus. This is the greatest gift I have ever been given. I do not attribute it to homeschool at all. But, in my faith, I am grateful for my sound Biblical education. This I do attribute to homeschool. I was taught the scriptures each day before I started mathematics. My history and science classes were based on the truth.

I was also protected from pitfalls I now see as destructive. My younger self would have been devastated by certain influences, temptations, and emotional struggles I avoided by being homeschooled. Thomson and Jang (2016) investigated the relationship between homeschool and underage drinking, and conclude:

> As expected, homeschool teens were less likely to drink and get drunk than public and, to a lesser extent, private school students partly because they are less likely to have deviant friends than public school

students, more likely to be subject to parental monitoring than private school students, and more likely to be religious in peer relations as well as beliefs and behaviors than both. (p. 296)

This is an example of how homeschool can be beneficial to students in a moral or religious way. The idea of being sheltered often has a negative connotation. I was sheltered. And I say when it's storming outside, underneath a rock isn't a bad place to be.

Many disagree with my religious views. People who think immersion in the existing culture is best won't find benefit from homeschooling in this regard. Most parents desire to teach their children what they think is true and to act the way they think is right. Homeschool is the surest way of doing this. Benoit (2011) writes, "Homeschooling provides parents a level playing field, a safe place from which to interact with their children about the proper way to distinguish between important and unimportant information and identify the often one-sided methods by which information is delivered," (p. 25). Some may use homeschooling to shut children out of society and teach them to hate all outside ideas. This is not common. I learned by instruction what my parents believe, and I learned by example how to receive outside ideas. But I believe and discern on my own. The point is homeschooling allows parents to be the primary influence on a student. Benoit (2011) says, "Homeschooling reinforces the idea that parents should be the first and most important filter, one that protects their children from ideological indoctrination and the one-sided, politicized spin of the contemporary classroom," (p.25). Whether or not this is a benefit to students again depends on their views. For me it was beneficial.

Conclusions

I was taught at home from first grade through high

school. My mom and dad and older brother taught me how to learn and how to live. I was loved abundantly.

I am in college now, and I see how beneficial my education was. Without knowing it, I was raised with high academic standards. Perfectionism upheld by gentleness and reward marked my school. Love motivated hard work to become my practice. Both common and uncommon experiences highlighted my life. I enjoyed sports, parties, fellowship, and travel all with the guidance and friendship of my family. I learned social skills from my parents instead of from my peers. I was brought up in a safe environment, protected from emotional and spiritual dangers. My parents taught me the truth every day in conjunction with my schoolwork.

Research shows homeschoolers do well in academics. Homeschooling could be a cause of scholastic success. Homeschoolers have access to extra-curricular activities. We enjoy sports, games, and clubs as well as projects and travel unlimited by school schedules. Research also indicates excellent social development in homeschoolers. According to professional opinion, homeschool allows students to be most influenced by their parents.

Homeschool is beneficial to students. It was for me. It is for most people who try it. Learning is most comfortable and most efficient when it is individual and customized. People work hardest and happiest for instructors who love them.

67042373R00097

Made in the USA
Lexington, KY
31 August 2017